PELICAN BOOKS

SUICIDE AND
ATTEMPTED SUICIDE

Professor Erwin Stengel was born in Vienna
in 1902 and educated there. He qualified in
the University of Vienna in 1926, did
research in anatomy and pathology of the
nervous system, neurology, and psychiatry,
and trained in psychoanalysis. He was a
lecturer in the Vienna University Department
of Neurology and Psychiatry at the height
of its fame. He left Austria in 1938 and
held a number of research and clinical posts
in England and Scotland, among them
Reader in Psychiatry in the University of
London and Consultant Psychiatrist at the
Bethlem Royal and the Maudsley Hospital.
In 1956 he was appointed to the newly
established Chair of Psychiatry in the
University of Sheffield. He was Professor
Emeritus from October 1967 until his
death in 1973.

Professor Stengel was President of the
International Association for Suicide Prevention.
He published numerous studies of problems in
neurology and psychiatry. He began research
into suicide and attempted suicide in 1950,
and in 1958 published a monograph, *Attempted
Suicide*, jointly with N. G. Cook.

Erwin Stengel

Suicide and
Attempted Suicide

Penguin Books

Penguin Books Ltd, Harmondsworth, Middlesex, England
Penguin Books, 625 Madison Avenue, New York, New York 10022, U.S.A.
Penguin Books Australia Ltd, Ringwood, Victoria, Australia
Penguin Books Canada Ltd, 2801 John Street, Markham, Ontario, Canada L3R 1B4
Penguin Books (N.Z.) Ltd, 182–190 Wairau Road, Auckland 10, New Zealand

First published 1964
Reprinted 1966, 1967
Revised edition 1970
Reprinted 1971
Reprinted with revisions 1973
Reprinted 1975, 1977, 1980, 1983

Made and printed in Singapore by
Richard Clay (S.E.Asia) Pte Ltd
Set in Monotype Times

Contents

Editorial Foreword   7

Author's Foreword   10

1   Introduction   13

Part 1 Suicide

2   The Statistics   19

3   The Act of Suicide   38

4   Motives and Causes   46

5   Suicide and Mental Disorders   58

6   The Attitudes of Society to Suicide   65

Part II Attempted Suicide

7   The Suicidal Attempt as a Behaviour Pattern, and its Definition   77

8   The Statistics   88

9   Methods used in Suicidal Attempts   92

10 Cohort Studies 94

11 For and Against Self-Destruction 100

12 The Psychological and Social Effects of
Attempted Suicide 105

13 The Psychodynamics of the Attempt 113

Part III Suicidal Acts Irrespective of Outcome

14 The Psychodynamics of Suicidal Acts 121

15 Prevention and Prophylaxis 137

Bibliography 151

Index 155

Editorial Foreword
to the First Edition

The act of suicide, which represents both personal unhappiness and the implied belief that the victim's fellow-men are powerless to remedy his condition, can never be viewed with indifference. In some cultures, including our own, it has been indignantly repudiated as an act of impiety: as recently as 1823 a London suicide was buried at a cross-roads in Chelsea with a stake through his body, and right up to 1961, in England and Wales, survivors of a suicidal attempt were liable to criminal prosecution. These attitudes of abhorrence and retaliation have now given way to a realization that anyone who tries to take his own life must be either sick or in great distress and certainly in need of medical and social assistance.

For well over a hundred years it has been known that suicide is a social phenomenon as well as a private act. The rate of suicide varies greatly from country to country (from just over three per 100,000 in the Republic of Ireland in 1961, to figures seven times greater in Austria, eight times greater in Hungary and twelve times greater in West Berlin) and yet in each separate country the rate remains remarkably consistent from year to year, except when some major event such as a world war supervenes. This has prompted sociologists, from the time of Morselli and Durkheim to the present day, to try to identify some of the cultural and environmental factors which are responsible for this consistency. It has to be remembered, however, that social influences can influence not only the act of suicide, but also its public recognition.

Professor Stengel is a psychiatrist who has made important contributions to this field of study. As a research worker, his first concern is to ascertain facts and figures as accurately as he can. He warns us against accepting national statistics of suicide at their face value – for example, differences in the accuracy of ascertainment are believed to be the chief reason for the very large discrepancies between the suicide rates of England, Scotland, and the Republic of Ireland. If this can happen within the British Isles, there must be even larger sources of error in the figures published by countries of widely differing levels of technical development. Professor Stengel draws attention to the very wide range of attitudes shown towards self-destruction in different cultural and religious traditions; but when he comes to discuss the causes of suicide he draws upon a few careful inquiries which have been carried out on accurately defined populations within particular countries. Important observations of this kind have been made upon the multi-racial populations of Hong Kong, Singapore, and Ceylon; but most of the research has come from northern Europe and the U.S.A.

We are reminded that in England and Wales approximately 5,500 people commit suicide each year, and six to ten times that number make a suicidal attempt from which they recover. This is a disquietingly large figure. At first sight it seems surprising that so many people should reach the point of despair at a time when our material prosperity is greater than ever before, but the experience of other countries, such as Denmark and Sweden, shows a similar paradox; and within our own society poverty as such is not associated with a raised suicide rate. On the contrary it is members of certain professional groups – doctors, dentists, lawyers and retired army officers – who show the highest rates. A recent editorial annotation in the *British Medical Journal* began: 'This month and every month a doctor in Great Britain, on the average, will kill himself.' It went on to point out that more than one in every fifty male doctors takes his own life.

Suicide is mainly a problem of middle and later life, but even among university students it is a problem to be reckoned with, coming second only to accidents as a cause of death. Attempted suicide, on the other hand, has many special aspects which have been neglected hitherto. Professor Stengel showed in his earlier monograph on this subject, and reminds us again in this book, that there are important differences, both in the persons involved and in the attendant medical and social circumstances, between those who make a suicidal attempt and those who actually kill themselves. He succeeds in doing justice to the complexity of motives which lie behind every such act, motives which are seldom clearly formulated by the actor himself, because some of their elements lie in the unconscious.

Research into the causes of suicidal acts is carried out, as is any form of medical research, not only in order to add to knowledge but also to promote informed preventive measures. Professor Stengel's book will be of real assistance to anyone, whether doctor, social worker, or layman, who encounters this problem. Throughout the world, it is becoming appreciated that crises of despair which may lead to suicide are not uncommon in modern urban society. Traditionally, the principal 'helping agencies' in the community have been doctors and clergymen, but since the war an important new organization has come into being: the Telephone Samaritans. In many cities, and in many countries, these voluntary groups of clergy and trained laymen provide a service of advice and help, available by means of a telephone call at any hour of day or night. This is an important preventive measure, which reveals a great many minor causes of bewilderment, financial crisis, and marital disharmony, in addition to the unfortunates who are in imminent danger of suicide. Professor Stengel pays tribute to the Samaritan movement in his review of what can be done to cope with these problems. Throughout his book, it is apparent that he writes not only as a statistician and a research worker, but even more as a clinician whose curiosity about the events he describes is always tempered by a concern for the individuals who are involved in them.

G. M. CARSTAIRS

Author's Foreword to the Revised Edition

This book, which appeared first in 1964 and was reprinted with only a few minor amendments in 1966 and 1967, was on the whole well received. This second and expanded edition takes account of new work published during the last six years. It also endeavours to clarify some misconceptions which arose from the way in which the material was presented in the first edition, especially from the separate discussion of suicide and of attempted suicide. The significance of the appeal effect in the motivations of suicidal acts, too, tended to be misunderstood.

It is hoped that the book will continue to be of help to all those who are interested in this peculiarly human type of behaviour and its prevention.

E.S.

Acknowledgements

I am indebted to the editor of the *British Medical Journal* for permission to reproduce Table 5, to Messrs Chapman and Hall for permission to reproduce tables from *Suicide in London* by P. Sainsbury and from *Attempted Suicide* by E. Stengel and N. G. Cook.

My grateful thanks are due to Mrs Eileen Judge for secretarial assistance and unfailing patience throughout the work and to Mrs Brenda Stockley for her help with the final version of the first edition. I am indebted to Mrs Audrey Lynn for secretarial help with the new revision.

E.S.

1   Introduction

Suicide appears to be the most personal action an individual can take, yet social relationships play an important part in its causation and it has a profound social impact. While it seems to aim solely at destroying the self, it is also an act of aggression against others. The study of suicide illustrates that human action, however personal, is also interaction with other people, and that the individual cannot be understood in isolation from his social matrix. Throughout the ages suicide has been pondered by priests, poets, and philosophers. Today it is a subject of scientific study and it will be presented as such in this book. First, what are the facts?

In recent years between 4,000 and 5,000 people have died through suicide in Great Britain annually and about 20,000 in the United States. These figures constitute suicide rates of eight to ten per 100,000 of the general population. Non-fatal suicidal acts, i.e. suicidal attempts, have been estimated to be eight to ten times as numerous as suicides. Neither the triumphs of scientific medicine nor the rise in the standard of living have reduced the incidence of suicidal acts. They have, on the contrary, tended to increase it.

Suicide is a specifically human problem. Any animal can die by disease and can be destroyed intentionally or accidentally by an outside agency. But, as far as we know, only man can will his death and kill himself. It is true that some animals are known under certain circumstances to behave in a manner which results in their death, but there is no evidence that this behaviour is associated with the wish to die. Nobody has proved that the faithful dog who starves to death on his master's grave knows that the master is dead, nor is there any evidence that the lemmings, which plunge into the sea to their death, do so from an urge to self-destruction. Self-destructive behaviour not associated with the idea of death is not suicide. At some stage of evolution man must have discovered that he can kill not only animals and fellowmen but also himself. It can be assumed that life has never since been the same to him. It would make a tremendous difference to man's attitude to life and death if the possibility of others and indeed of oneself committing suicide should cease to exist. It is difficult to imagine man entirely without this potential.

Suicide is ubiquitous. The belief that it does not occur in primitive societies has proved to be mistaken: there is no period in history without records of suicides. There are few if any individuals to whom the idea of suicide has never occurred.

Clear definition of terms is essential in this field. 'Suicide' means not only 'the act of taking one's life', but also 'one who dies from his own hand', and 'one who attempts or has a tendency to commit suicide'. Figuratively used, it refers to behaviour of individuals or groups which may bring about their own destruction. Ruskin had this in mind when he spoke of 'the suicide of Greece'. The quotations are from the *Oxford English Dictionary* which faithfully records the varied usage of the term in everyday language and literature. Suicide, then, has at least four different though related connotations, each of which refers to self-destruction.

The use of the same word for the act and its victim may be objectionable, but is relatively harmless in this case. It is in keeping with the habit of the clinician to employ the same term for the disease and the person suffering from it. However, to use suicide for both the fatal and the non-fatal act of self-injury is bound to lead to confusion. The same applies to the indiscriminate use of the term for self-damaging behaviour not consciously aimed at death.

Suicide means the fatal, and *suicidal attempt* the non-fatal act of self-injury undertaken with more or less conscious self-destructive intent, however vague and ambiguous. The terms successful and unsuccessful suicide will not be used as they imply that death is the *only* aim of every suicidal act, a notion which has lately been challenged. Attempted suicide has only recently received serious attention. It used to be treated as merely bungled suicide, undeserving of special interest except as a symptom of mental disorder, but in fact it requires special study because it presents many important problems of its own which do not arise from suicide.

Part I of this book deals with suicide, Part II with attempted suicide, Part III with the problems common to all suicidal acts.

Part I

Suicide

The Statistics

Suicides have been registered in Europe and in North America since the beginning of the nineteenth century, and for even longer in some countries. To compare their incidence in different periods and places it is necessary to calculate the suicide death rates for a certain proportion of the population. Table 1 is an extract from a statistical report of the World Health Organization (W. H. O.). It shows the fluctuations of the suicide death rates per 100,000 in a number of countries over a period of ten years. In almost half the countries listed the increase was slight to moderate. In the remainder there was no change or a slight decrease.

The 1955 rates were over twenty in Austria, Denmark, Hungary, Japan, West Berlin, Switzerland, and East Germany. They were between fifteen and twenty in Finland, France, Sweden, and Western Germany. Rates of ten to fourteen were found in Australia, Belgium, South Africa, England and Wales, the United States, and New Zealand. The lowest rates were recorded in Egypt, the Republic of Ireland, Northern Ireland and among the Negro populations of the United States and South Africa. The 1965 rates showed a decline in Austria, Denmark, Japan, Sweden and Switzerland, and an increase in several other countries. Only in West Berlin was there a marked rise.

The figures presented in Table 1 are the suicide death rates per 100,000 of the general population comprising all age groups. They are not identical with the suicide rates in the strict sense, which comprise only the suicide death rates per 100,000 of the general population aged 15 and over. The lower age groups are excluded because they contribute hardly anything to the suicide figures. The inclusion of a large section of the population which is irrelevant for this particular problem tends to give a somewhat misleading, i.e. an unduly favourable picture, by diluting the population at risk. The inaccuracy caused by the loss to the national statistics of a tiny number of child suicides is negligible. In 1965, for instance, the registered number of suicides committed in England and Wales under the age of 15 was 3, out of a total of 5,161. In 1966, the corresponding number was 4. These cases are of course taken into consideration in general psychopathological studies.

Table 2 has been taken from a special W.H.O. publication on suicide. It presents the suicide rates proper. They are considerably higher than the suicide death rates for all ages (Table 1) and give a truer picture of the size of the problem than the former. The table also avoids possible fallacies by using averages from three successive years instead of picking out single years. It also shows the variations of the sex difference in the suicide rates of different countries. The male/female ratio is lowest in Japan, Israel, and England and Wales.

It is tempting to draw facile conclusions from differences in national suicide rates. Sweden has some time ago been the subject of benevolent though not unbiased attention. First, President Eisenhower singled out the Swedish suicide rate as a warning of what happened to a country with a leftish government. He must have been unacquainted with the even higher suicide rates of some other countries whose political complexion was more to his liking. Hendin, an American psychoanalyst, went to Sweden to study the causes of the high suicide rate. He carefully examined individuals who had made suicidal attempts and concluded that the Swedes' attitudes to love and work and their way of bringing up their children were responsible for the high rate. His personality profiles would have fitted British subjects just as well. This type of clinical study of national differences carries no conviction because it is not suited methodologically to the problem it tries to solve.

Suicide rates tend to understate the truth, even in countries

Table 1. Suicide death rates per 100,000 population (from *World Health Statistics Report 21,* No. 6, Geneva : W. H. O., 1968)

	1955	1965
Australia	10.3	14.9
Austria	23.4	22.8
Belgium	13.5	15.0
Czechoslovakia		21.5
Denmark	23.3	19.5
Egypt	0.2	
Finland	19.9	19.8
France	15.9	15.0
Germany		
W. Germany	19.2	20.0
W. Berlin	34.3	41.3
Democratic Republic	27.7	
Hungary	20.6	29.8
Israel	5.5	6.6
Italy	6.6	5.4
Japan	25.2	14.7
Netherlands	6.0	6.9
New Zealand	9.0	9.1
Norway	7.4	7.7
Republic of Ireland	2.3	1.8
S. Africa (Europeans)	11.3	14.1*
(Africans)		4.3*
Spain	5.5	4.8
Sweden	17.8	18.9
Switzerland	21.6	18.4
United Kingdom		
England and Wales	11.3	10.8
Scotland	7.7	8.8
N. Ireland	3.3	4.8
United States (all races)	10.2	11.1
White	11.1	
Negroes	3.8	

*1961

Table 2. Death rates from suicide in 1952–54 and 1961–63 (yearly average) for each sex and both sexes, from 15 years of age, per 100,000 population (from *Prevention of Suicide*, Public Health Paper No. 35, Geneva : W. H. O.,1968)

Country	Period	Yearly average rates			
		Both sexes	Male	Female	Excess male*
Australia	1952–54	14.9	21.9	7.7	
	1961–63	19.6	27.0	12.2	221
Austria	1952–54	29.9	43.0	19.2	
	1961–63	28.3	42.0	16.9	249
Czechoslovakia	1961–63	28.2	40.9	16.5	248
Denmark	1952–54	31.9	43.6	20.6	
	1961–63	24.2	32.4	16.2	200
England & Wales	1952–54	13.8	18.5	9.5	
	1961–63	15.1	18.3	12.2	150
Finland	1952–54	25.8	43.6	9.9	
	1961–63	29.0	47.7	12.3	388
France	1952–54	20.3	32.6	9.4	
	1961–63	20.7	32.3	10.0	323
Germany	1952–54	23.6	33.7	15.1	
(Federal Republic)	1961–64	24.1	33.3	16.2	206
Hungary	1961–63	33.9	48.9	20.3	241
Israel (Jewish population)	1961–63	10.1	11.9	8.2	145
Italy	1952–54	6.4	11.9	4.8	
	1961–63	7.1	10.2	4.2	243
Japan	1952–54	31.4	38.8	24.5	
	1961–63	24.7	29.0	20.6	141
Norway	1952–54	9.8	15.1	4.6	
	1961–63	10.0	15.7	4.5	349
Scotland	1952–54	7.5	10.7	4.6	
	1961–63	11.4	15.2	8.1	188
Sweden	1952–54	23.4	35.2	10.7	
	1961–63	21.7	32.0	11.6	276
Switzerland	1952–54	28.8	44.9	14.3	
	1961–63	23.3	33.9	13.2	257
United States	1952–54	14.1	22.8	5.9	
	1961–63	15.6	24.0	7.7	312

* Number of male suicides for every 100 female suicides.

with a long scientific tradition of vital statistics. According to the most recent book by Louis I. Dublin, who is the leading statistician on this subject, the number of suicides in the United States is most probably higher by one fourth to one third than recorded. This means that in 1966 it is more likely to have been 27,000 than 21,281 per year, which was the official figure. In the United States, as in this country, the suicide figures are largely derived from coroners' verdicts which are sometimes inconclusive, even in cases where the medical evidence for suicide is adequate. The criteria of proof required for a coroner's verdict differ from those of a post-mortem diagnosis of the cause of death.

The suicide figures for Great Britain are probably no more reliable than those for the United States. But there are other factors which tend to falsify the suicide rates. In Roman Catholic and Moslem countries a verdict of suicide is such a disgrace for the deceased and his family that it is avoided wherever possible. This is why the very low suicide rates of the Republic of Ireland and Egypt are suspect. In many countries the methods of registration leave much to be desired. This factor might be partly or wholly responsible for the difference between the suicide rates of England and Wales and of Scotland. The latter has been consistently lower than the former by one half to one third. Dr Neil Kessel, working in Edinburgh, has checked on the recording of an unselected sample of known cases of suicide in Scotland and found only half of them so recorded.* Another source of underestimation is the difficulty in some cases of distinguishing between suicide and accident as cause of death.

A world wide survey carried out with the help of a questionnaire by Stengel and Farberow revealed a great variety of methods and criteria of certification of suicide. Legislation and social and religious attitudes concerning suicidal acts varied greatly. The authors recommended the introduction of uniform certification procedures and of operational criteria for case finding, but they were under no illusion that this would be easy to achieve.

The need for caution in the evaluation of national differences has now been officially recognized. In the introduction to the

* Personal communication.

Suicide Mortality Statistics published by the World Health Organization in 1968 the following warning was included:

The true incidence of suicide is hard to ascertain. Varying methods of certifying causes of death, different registration and coding procedures, and other factors affect the extent and completeness of coverage making international comparisons impracticable. However, the trend of mortality and the groups of population at relatively high risk for the same country may point to fields needing further investigation.

For all these reasons the study of disparities and fluctuations of the suicide rates in the same country is of greater scientific value than comparisons between different countries, unless one is satisfied that the figures are really comparable; and they are not unless the statistical data are equally reliable. However, it is obvious that highly industrialized and prosperous countries tend to have comparatively high suicide rates.

England and Wales and the white population of the United States have almost identical suicide rates. They compare favourably with those of some other countries. The notably low rate among the American Negro population will be discussed later.

The British suicide figures have been fluctuating during the last few decades, having decreased from about 5,100 a year pre-war (1936–9) to about 3,500 during the last war. In 1949 they increased to 4,721. Table 3 shows the suicide figures for England and Wales for the ten-year period 1952–61 presented by the Minister of Health in a written answer to a question put in the House of Commons (Hansard, 19 November 1962, p. 93). Two features stand out in this table. Firstly, the increase of the total and, secondly, the relatively higher increase in the number of females. However, these figures exaggerate the increase because they do not take into consideration the growth of the population. The Minister ought to have quoted the rates per 100,000 which do not show a marked increase. Table 4 has been taken from the same W. H. O. report as Table 1. The suicide rate for England and Wales has fallen since 1963.

The post-war suicide rate per 100,000 in England and Wales irrespective of sex, has not yet reached the pre-war level. However, if the two sexes are considered separately the picture is

Table 3. Suicide figures for England and Wales 1952-61

	1952	1953	1954	1955	1956	1957	1958	1959	1960	1961
Male	2800	3021	3179	3075	3196	3188	3145	3115	3071	3034
Female	1543	1746	1861	1955	2084	2141	2123	2093	2060	2182
Total	4343	4767	5040	5030	5280	5329	5268	5208	5131	5216

different: while the male rate has continued rather low, the female rate has increased steadily. The graph shown overleaf presents the fluctuations of the suicide rates for England and Wales for each sex during sixty years from 1901.

Table 4. Suicide death rates in England and Wales per 100,000 population by sex, 1951–61

	1951	1952	1953	1954	1955	1956	1957	1958	1959	1960	1961
Total*	10.2	9.9	10.8	11.4	11.3	11.8	11.8	11.7	11.5	11.3	11.3
Male	13.4	13.2	14.2	14.9	14.3	14.9	14.6	14.6	14.2	13.9	13.5
Female	7.2	6.8	7.6	8.1	8.4	9.0	9.2	9.1	8.9	8.7	9.1

*Refers to people irrespective of sex.

No one single cause or group of causes can account for the level of suicide rates. Many factors are at work at the same time. Suicide rates, for example, have been found to be positively correlated with the following factors: *male sex, increasing age, widowhood, single and divorced state, childlessness, high density of population, residence in big towns, a high standard of living, economic crisis, alcohol and addictive drugs consumption, a broken home in childhood, mental disorder, and physical illness.*

Among factors inversely related to the suicide rates are *female sex, youth, low density of population (though it must not be too low), rural occupation, religious devoutness, the married state, a large number of children, membership of the lower socio-economic classes, war.*

These correlations have been found in most Western communities and possibly do not obtain in other types of society. The two lists represent broad generalizations. Some factors, such as those pertaining to living standards, have not the same effect in all age groups. There is nothing permanent in the correlations,

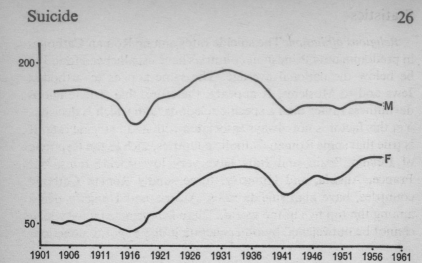

1901 1906 1911 1916 1921 1926 1931 1936 1941 1946 1951 1956 1961

The graph shows the trend of the suicide rates for England and Wales during 1901–61 (from the Registrar General's Statistical Review of England and Wales for the year 1961. Part III, Commentary). M = male, F = female. There was a marked decline, more pronounced in the male than in the female population, during the two world wars. The increase of the suicide rates since 1942 has been negligible among males but very marked among females. The post-war female suicide rate has risen above the level it had reached before the last war, while the male rate has remained well below it.

and some differences between factors making for an increase and factors making for a decrease in the suicide rates are gradually being levelled out. This applies, for instance, to *sex*. It is still true that the majority of suicides are male, but during the last few decades the gap between men and women who have killed themselves has been narrowing in many countries. Tables 2 and 3 illustrate this trend. In some recent years females have been in the majority among the suicides in several English cities. The increase in the female population, due to the fact that women live longer than men, is partly responsible for this change. Hartelius, a Swedish student of suicide, has blamed it on three modern developments which have profoundly changed women's life, i.e. urbanization, secularization, and emancipation.

Religious affiliation. The suicide rates among Roman Catholics in predominantly Protestant countries have usually been found to be below the national average. The same applies to orthodox Jews and to Moslems. It appears, therefore, that it is religious devoutness rather than a specific religious faith which is decisive. Yet this factor is not always associated with a low suicide rate. It is true that some Roman Catholic countries, such as the Republic of Ireland, Spain, and Italy have very low suicide rates, but France, Austria, and Hungary, three solidly Roman Catholic countries, have high suicide rates, Austria and Hungary being among the top five in the world. There is no single factor which cannot be outweighed by others acting in the opposite direction.

Age. Contrary to the popular belief, which associates suicide with frustrated love and 'poor moral fibre', the majority of the people who kill themselves are elderly and many of them are physically sick. Their average age is in the late fifties. One of the reasons why highly developed and prosperous countries have higher suicide rates than underdeveloped and poor countries is that the expectation of life is far longer in the former than in the latter. The great medical discoveries of our time have benefited mainly the younger age groups. The diseases of middle and old age still remain to be conquered. Thus, more people are enabled to become old and sick today than were in the past. This is why scientific medicine, improved medical care, and material prosperity tend to increase the suicide rates. A low expectation of life of the general population makes for a low incidence of suicide. A low suicide rate may conceal more human misery than is revealed by a high rate. The over-representation of the older age groups in prosperous communities is not the only cause for their high suicide rates. One suspects that there are other causes of a sociological and psychological nature. The inevitable social and psychological isolation of old age is accentuated by the tendency of the family group in our society to break up into its smallest units. Prosperity has favoured this trend. For two or three generations of a family to live together under the same roof is felt to be an intolerable hardship. Living in a large family group, which is still a feature of social life in the less prosperous parts of the world, has no doubt certain disadvantages. But freedom from restrictive family ties and disturbing family tensions has often to be paid for by social isolation.

Social isolation is the common denominator of a number of factors correlated with a high suicide rate. While marriage and a big family seem to confer a certain immunity against suicide, they appear to stimulate homicide which is only too often a family crime. This statistical relationship between suicide, homicide, and the married state ·supports the contention of the psychoanalysts that both suicide and homicide are manifestations of uncontrolled aggressive impulses and differ only in their choice of objects. Similar considerations concerning the psychological dynamics and economics of aggression may help to understand why suicide rates invariably decline in time of war. It is a melancholy thought that marriage and the family should be such effective substitutes for conditions of war, as far as the direction of aggressive impulses is concerned.

The higher incidence of suicide in *urban communities* has been attributed to the greater risk of social isolation and the anonymity of life in the big cities, compared with the closely-knit village community. As a rule the suicide rates are proportionate to the size of the city. Exceptions to this rule require special explanation. Recently a striking discrepancy between the suicide rates of two industrial cities in the North of England was investigated by Stengel and Cook. Paradoxically, the smaller of the two, which had only one fifth of the population of the other city, had over a considerable period a suicide rate far in excess of the national average and several times that of the bigger city. A comparative study of the relevant factors revealed that a large number of young people had emigrated from the smaller city owing to the decline of the local industry. As a result, the older age groups were grossly over-represented in the population, with a consequent increase of the death rates in general and the suicide rates in particular. No similar change in the age composition of the population had taken place in the bigger city. There is evidence that the excessive suicide rate in West Berlin (Table 1, p. 21) is at least partly due to emigration from the younger age groups and subsequent over-representation of the middle-aged and aged.

Suicide rates may differ not only from city to city but also in different parts of the same urban area. Investigations carried out independently in Chicago and in London showed that the suicide rates were highest in those parts where the population was shifting, i.e. in districts with many hotels and lodging houses, and also in the most prosperous sections of the city. According to Sainsbury, the prosperous western suburbs of London had a much higher incidence of suicides than the solid working-class boroughs in the eastern part of the city. Bloomsbury, with its many hotels and boarding houses, had a high rate. Twenty-seven per cent of the suicides in London had been living alone, whereas only seven per cent of the general population lived alone. The foreign born were over-represented among the suicides. Social isolation, social mobility, and social disorganization measured by the divorce and illegitimacy rates proved to be significantly correlated with the incidence of suicide. The higher social classes were over-represented among the suicides while the lower classes were under-represented compared with their proportions in the general population. A more recent study in Los Angeles failed to show a difference between the suicide rates of the various social classes. Possibly there are no such discrepancies where the living standard of the whole community, including even those out of work, is high. In 1957, when the study was carried out, the population of Los Angeles was five million, with a suicide rate of 15.4 per 100,000.

Social class expressed by grouping of occupations has been found to be an important factor in suicide in this country and elsewhere. The suicide rate has in the last few decades been highest among people engaged in professional and managerial occupations (class I) followed as a rule by that of businessmen and executives (class II). Medical and dental practitioners are among the professional groups with the highest suicide rates:

they have more than double the rate of a comparable sample of the general population. Ready access to poison and greater awareness of disease may be partly responsible. Classes III (skilled workers) and IV (partly skilled) have low suicide rates. The rates among unskilled workers (class V) are usually higher than in classes III and IV, sometimes as high as those of class II. Married women are classified by their husbands' occupations. These class gradients are not static. In the twenties of this century class II had the highest suicide rate. In old age the upper classes are no longer over-represented. Table 5, for instance, shows that

Table 5. Standardized Mortality Ratio for suicide per million among males in various social classes by broad age groups. England and Wales 1949–53 (from the Registrar General's Decennial Supplement 1961)

Social class	20–64 years	65 years and over
I	140	98
II	113	89
III	89	102
IV	92	87
V	117	120

in England and Wales the suicide rate among old men was highest in class V during 1949–53. The lower frequency of suicide among the well-to-do classes in old age may be due to their greater economic stability compared with the old age pensioners.

In the United States the suicide rates of the first four classes have not differed substantially in recent years. The highest suicide mortality was found in group V. This may be due to the high rate of unemployment and the threat of loss of work in the United States especially among the unskilled working class.

Suicides among university students have received considerable publicity in recent years. The suicide rates are higher than in the corresponding age groups of the general population. Table 6 illustrates this, and also the remarkable differences between the 'ancient' universities, i.e. Oxford and Cambridge, where the rates were five to six times in excess of expectation, and a group of provincial universities where they were much lower though still excessive. University College, London, had an intermediate position. Although the actual figures are small they have given rise to much concern and speculation. No corresponding figures from American universities have come to hand except for Yale University, which had a suicide rate of thirteen. This is excessive for this age group but not as high as at Oxford or Cambridge. The high incidence of suicide among university students and the disparities among them are of general interest because they exemplify the problems arising from differences of suicide rates in comparable groups.

It is not surprising that the student population as a whole should show a relatively high incidence of suicides. There is at least one social factor by which the students differ from their contemporaries, i.e. the excess of unmarried individuals; but this fails to explain why the ancient universities should be at a disadvantage. Several other factors have been incriminated. One of them is, in the late Sir Alan Rook's opinion, the college system which 'breaks the university into a number of self-contained somewhat isolated communities'. The high academic standards and the lack of a rigid schedule of work are also thought to be important. Students in Oxford and Cambridge are left to themselves more than students in other universities, as far as the organization of their studies is concerned. Possibly the size of student population is also a factor. The number of students at Oxford and Cambridge is two to three times that of the average British provincial university. Larger urban populations have as a rule higher suicide rates than smaller ones. The view has also been expressed that Oxford and Cambridge have a greater attraction for eccentric and therefore more vulnerable personalities than other universities.

F. Zweig's recent survey of Oxford and Manchester students demonstrates significant differences between the two universities. It can be taken that the Oxford sample is also representative of Cambridge and that the Manchester sample typifies the English provincial ('red brick') universities. Fifty-five per cent of the Manchester students came from skilled working-class or lower

Table 6. Student Suicides in England and Wales. (Modified from *Brit. Med. J. 1*, p. 600, 1959.) The suicide figures are averages from periods ranging from 8.5 to 10 years

Group		Population yearly average	No. of Suicides	Annual Rate per 100,000
Cambridge 1948–58	Men	5,950	13	21.8
	Women	630	1	
Oxford 1957	Men	5,250	16	30.5
	Women	800		
Seven British universities	Men	15,000	10	8.5
	Women	5,000		
University College London 1957	Men	2,500	3	17.1
	Women	1,000	1	
England and Wales Age 15–19 1948–56	Men	1,302,000	331	2.8
	Women	1,389,000	134	1.1
England and Wales Age 20–24 1948–56	Men	1,394,000	767	6.1
	Women	1,462,000	282	2.1

middle-class families as against only twenty-two per cent at Oxford. The corresponding figures for upper and upper middle-class together were five for Manchester and twenty-four for Oxford. Two thirds of the Manchester students could maintain close contact with their parents even in term time, since they either lived at home or were not far from home. For most of the Oxford students university life meant separation from home. To a large proportion of them, i.e. the public schoolboys, this was not a new experience. The proportion of students whose home was abroad was much higher at Oxford than at Manchester. Separation from home is both more common and more drastic among upper and upper middle-class youth than among young people belonging to other classes.

The discrepancy between the suicide rates of the two university populations might be related to the differences in class composition and in relation to home. The majority of the Manchester students came from the social classes with low suicide rates, while the majority of the Oxford students came from the classes which tend to be over-represented among suicides, at least in this country.

The excessive frequency of suicide among university students is not confined to the English speaking countries. Lungershausen in Bonn investigated the suicide rates among the students of the universities and kindred institutions of Nordrhein-Westfalen for the period 1958–65. The size of this population was 49,200 on the average, 20 per cent of them female. The total suicide rate in this group was 26.0 for *both sexes together*, well above that of the corresponding age group in the general population.

Cresswell and Smith have demonstrated a positive correlation between the male/female ratio and the suicide rate in British university populations. The higher this ratio was the higher was the rate, especially when the former could not be corrected by the presence of adequate numbers of young females in the environment. In this respect, Cambridge, a small town with a large university, sex ratio 9:1, was at a great disadvantage compared with Oxford, a medium sized industrial town whose university had a sex ratio of 5.6:1. The optimal ratio, in the authors' opinion, was 2.5:1. They regard an excessive discrepancy in the ratio of the two sexes as evidence of social disintegration.

The incidence of mental illness among students in general is, according to Kidd and Caldbeck-Meenan, probably no higher than in a comparable sample of the general population, but the demand for psychiatric treatment has been found to be greater among them than among their coevals working in business, industry or agriculture. Parnell and Skottowe of Oxford have reported that the annual first admission rate to mental hospitals among male students of that university was double that for the general population of similar age during 1952–6. No conclusions about the incidence of mental illness can be drawn from such figures because one has to expect a higher admission rate from a section of the population which lives away from home. Some of the milder psychological disorders, especially the neuroses, do not seriously affect the efficiency of young people gainfully employed, but may undermine the working capacity of university students. Today most of the students in this country depend on public grants which they lose if they do not pass their examinations within strictly limited periods. Reasonable though these requirements are from the point of view of the authorities that give the grants, which may be foreign governments, they add enormously to the consequences of failure. Our time has been called 'the age of anxiety', and it seems that the student experiences more anxiety than young people working in other fields. F. Zweig writes about them: 'They struck me as old, laden with responsibilities, care and worries....' A self-evaluation test employed by Zweig indicated that pessimists were more common among Oxford than among Manchester students. Zweig advocated 'more concern with mental health' in the universities.

There is indeed a strong case for a mental-health service in all universities. It seems that society expects at the same time too much and too little of the university students. Too much, because to succeed they ought to work steadily and wisely during the period when they go through the turbulent final phases of social maturation; too little, because they are still looked upon as pupils who cannot play the same part in the community as many of their contemporaries who work in industry and trade. From the point of view of mental hygiene the increase in the proportion of married students is to be welcomed. This development has been very noticeable in the United States, where most universities provide married quarters for their students.

The above paragraph was written in 1963, before the beginning of the unrest in European universities. A great deal has been said and written about the causes of this social phenomenon. It has at any rate demonstrated an enormous amount of pent-up aggression. It is not surprising that a section of the population which harbours so much aggression should have a high incidence of suicide which is an aggressive act directed against the self as well as against others. It will take some time to test the hypothesis that an eruption of aggression against external objects will result in a decline of the suicide rate in this particular population.

The significance of *race* as a factor in suicide is uncertain although the suicide rates of coloured people have almost invariably been far below those of the whites. This is particularly noticeable in South Africa and in the United States, where the suicide rates among Negroes are only half those of the white population. However, the living conditions are nowhere the same for both races and it would therefore be unjustified to attribute the difference in suicide rates to racial predisposition. The same consideration applies to the difference in the homicide rates to which the American Negro contributes more than the white population. Here again we find an inverse relationship between suicide and homicide rates.

In rural Africa suicides are not registered in the same way as in the countries that keep records and no comparable data have been available until recently. However, this deficiency is being remedied in some places. A few years ago a team of American anthropologists, under the leadership of Paul Bohannan, carried out a field study on homicide and suicide among several tribes in Nigeria, Uganda, and Kenya. They found that the homicide rates among Africans were far below those of American Negroes and did not exceed the European rates. Information about suicide was more difficult to come by and the figures available varied considerably. In some tribes the suicide rates reached those of Western communities. Recently a Nigerian psychiatrist, Dr Asuni, reported on the incidence of suicide in his country. As in Europe, it was more frequent among males than among females. On the other hand, people living alone were less liable to kill themselves than people living with their families, and the incidence was higher in the country than in the cities. The suicide rate was lower than in any Western country, but it is doubtful whether the figures are comparable.

The factors underlying suicidal acts in Malaya and Hong Kong appear to be the same as those in Western and African populations. The suicide rate in Hong Kong, which has a large number of immigrants, has increased in recent years. According to Yap, the highest rates were found among low-income and low-prestige groups such as concubines. No generalizations about suicide among the Chinese can be made from the Hong Kong data because they are derived from a population with a very unusual composition.

*

The incidence of suicide shows regular *seasonal fluctuations*. Contrary to expectation, the peak seasons for suicide are not autumn and winter when nature is at its most depressing, but spring and early summer, when nature is at its best and life seems most worthwhile. The incidence of suicide gradually increases from January, reaches its peak in May or June and starts to decline in early July. Sometimes there is a minor peak in autumn. In the antipodes the corresponding months are December and early January. Various explanations for these seasonal fluctuations have been advanced, for example that the increasing temperature in late spring and early summer leads to greater excitability with a greater liability to suicide. If this was so the incidence of suicide ought to be higher in hot than in cool springs and summers, especially in countries with moderate climates. No such correlation has been established. Durkheim believed that with the increasing length of the day social life became more intense and suicide more frequent in consequence. This explanation is not convincing because in some respects social contacts are closer in winter. In fact, the seasonal increase of the suicide incidence is still mysterious. It has been suggested that it may be the manifestation of one of the rhythmical biological changes which play an important part in animal life although they are much less conspicuous in man. It has often been reported that depressive illness is more common in spring than in the rest of the year. This would partly account for the seasonal increase in the incidence of suicide, but there must be other factors also.

*

The suicide rate of England and Wales fell from 12 to 8 per 100,000 between 1963 and 1970. R. Fox related this fall to the intensification of the work of the Samaritans (see pp. 138–43), now the largest suicide prevention organization in the world. The number of their branches in the United Kingdom grew from 28 in 1961 to 115 in 1970, the number of new clients from 12,355 to 68,531, and the number of helpers from 6,537 to 12,832. However, just how much of the fall of the suicide rate in England and Wales was due to the Samaritans it is impossible to say because it coincided with another development, i.e. the disappearance of highly toxic domestic gas from most British households. It has either been detoxicated or replaced by non-toxic North Sea gas. Hassal and Trethowan attributed the steep decline of the suicide rate in Birmingham (population, 1 million) during the years 1963 and 1970 wholly to the progressive detoxication of domestic gas. Coal gas poisoning used to be the most frequent single cause of death by suicide (Table 7). In 1961 the number of people who killed themselves by this method in England and Wales was 2,379 (5·1 per cent per 100,000); in 1969 it was 790 (1·6 per cent). There was a similar drop in Scotland and an even steeper one in the Netherlands where North Sea gas was introduced first (*World Health Statistics Report 25*, No. 8, 1972).

3   The Act of Suicide

There is a limited number of typical methods of suicide the choice of which depends partly on their availability. In Great Britain, where possession of firearms without a special licence is illegal, suicides by shooting are rare, while they are common in the United States where such restrictions either do not exist or are ignored. However, availability alone does not decide the choice of method. If it did, drowning or jumping from high places would be at the top of the list of methods almost everywhere.

Table 7. Methods of suicide per 1,000 deaths, 1955 and 1965, England and Wales (from *World Health Statistics Report 21,* No. 6, Geneva : W.H.O.,1968)

Method	Male 1955	1965	Female 1955	1965
1. Analgesics and narcotics	79	246	182	486
2. Other solid or liquid poison	29	24	22	19
3. Domestic gas	412	335	553	322
4. Other gases	13	48	1	7
5. Hanging and strangulation	187	134	64	55
6. Drowning	92	60	106	66
7. Firearms and explosives	71	63	5	4
8. Cutting and piercing instruments	53	21	11	5
9. Jumping from high places	19	18	29	17
10 Other agents	43	50	26	19

Table 7 shows the proportions of the various methods per 1,000 deaths by suicide in England and Wales in the years 1955 and 1965. The classification is the one adopted by the World Health Organization. The first category (analgesics and narcotics) includes the aspirin type of drug, with or without codeine, all hypnotics and the tranquillizers, the use of which for this purpose has greatly increased of late. Suicidal deaths by the aspirin type of drug form only a small fraction of this group.

If one divides the methods into poisoning, i.e. the first four, and fatal injuries, it becomes clear that in both sexes the majority of suicidal deaths belonged to the first group. In 1955, 53 per cent of the men and 75 per cent of the women had poisoned themselves. Of the other methods, hanging, shooting and the use of instruments were definitely more common among men than among women, while the opposite applied to drowning and falling from high places. Among the poisons, domestic gas was by far the most commonly used. By 1965 the picture had undergone some striking changes. Sixty-five per cent of the men and 82 per cent of the women had died by poisoning. The increase in the use of this group of methods was associated with a more or less marked decline in the frequency of the other methods, the fall being most striking for hanging and strangulation. Among the methods of poisoning, those with painkilling drugs and narcotics had increased dramatically, 3 times in men and 2.6 times in women. The use of domestic gas had declined by one-fifth in men and by two-fifths in women. In women there had also been a fall in the use of all the other methods, most strikingly of drowning. The changes shown in the tables had developed progressively over the ten-year period. It is necessary to state this, because data concerning single years can be misleading if they are not in keeping with the trends observable over longer periods.

The fall in the use of toxic domestic gas in suicide is due to a decline in its availability (p. 37). The compensatory rise of the mortality rate by drug poisoning is probably due also to the preference for this method by suicidal individuals. Similar, though less dramatic, changes in the use of these methods have been observed in other countries, e.g. in France, Germany, Japan and the United States. These observations are in keeping with the enormous increase in suicidal attempts with drugs in Western countries.

These developments have caused much concern in the medical profession and among the lay public. A tightening up of the regulations governing the use of dangerous drugs has been suggested and the free availability of aspirin and similar analgesics without prescription has come in for criticism. There are many arguments in favour of measures which might halt the disconcerting increase in drug consumption. The increase in suicidal acts by poisoning is only one of them, and perhaps not the strongest, because that increase has not been associated with a rise in the suicide rate from all causes. In this country there has even been a marked decline in the suicide rates of both sexes in recent years for which data are available. It is therefore possible that the growing preference for drug poisoning as a method of suicide may, by reducing the use of other methods which are less amenable to treatment, result in a decline of the suicide rate as a whole.

Table 8. Methods of suicide per 1,000 deaths, 1955 and 1965, United States (from *World Health Statistics Report 21,* No. 6, Geneva: W. H. O., 1968).

Method	Male 1955	1965	Female 1955	1965
1. Analgesics and narcotics	29	59	145	312
2. Other solid or liquid poison	31	27	90	60
3. Domestic gas	14	6	35	9
4. Other gases	95	113	57	87
5. Hanging and strangulation	208	158	238	124
6. Drowning	29	20	72	43
7. Firearms and explosives	525	546	252	240
8. Cutting and piercing instruments	28	19	32	19
9. Jumping from high places	26	31	50	48
10. Other agents	15	20	31	59

While more people than previously have killed themselves with drugs in recent years, many more have survived suicidal acts than would have done if the use of domestic gas, hanging and drowning had not declined.

In the United States and Canada, similar trends can be observed, but firearms still rule supreme. Table 8 compares the use of methods in 1955 to 1965. Slightly more than half of the males and about a quarter of the females who committed suicide shot themselves. Hanging was the next popular method, poisoning being much less prominent. The almost negligible number of coal gas poisonings is obviously due to its unavailability. The fourth method of poisoning, i.e. by gases other than domestic gas, was more frequent than in England. The most important member of this category is the exhaust gas from motor cars. The American statistics, too, show that poisoning is preferred by women. Although the percentage figures are too low to make a serious impact, there has been a marked increase of poisonings with analgesics and hypnotics over the ten year period, the figures having doubled in men, and more than doubled in women. The increase of suicide by exhaust gases was slight. Suicides by hanging have gone down by a quarter in men and by almost one half in women, but there was no change in the proportion of suicides by shooting in either sex. It can be predicted that effective restrictions in the availability of firearms would result in an increased use of drugs, a higher percentage of suicidal deaths by poisoning, and possibly in a decline of suicide rate from all causes. There has been no significant change in the suicide rates of the United States since 1955.

Sceptics looking over Table 8 will observe that suicides by shooting and hanging are so prominent in the list because they are the two methods most difficult to conceal and to distort. They may well be right. The apparent rarity of suicide by poisoning in the United States is highly suspect. A recent survey of coroners' verdicts in California has shown that the proportion of suicide verdicts by poisoning shows a high variability from county to county.

Table 8 does not differentiate between whites and Negroes. The relevant data for the two races separately were not yet available. Significant differences in the use of methods have been observed. Table 9 compares the methods most frequently employed by the two races, but does not differentiate between the sexes. It shows that Negroes use firearms even more than the whites, but the suicide rates for poisoning and hanging are lower among them that among the whites. The preference for the most violent method of suicide by the American Negro is in keeping with the higher incidence of crimes of violence among them. There is evidence that these differences are not primarily racial. The patterns of suicide of the American Negroes approximate the more to those of his white fellow citizens the more their way of life becomes similar to that of the white population. In Western Nigeria the order of frequency of the methods of suicide was: hanging, shooting, drowning, poisoning, wounding for males; hanging, poisoning, drowning, wounding for females. It was similar among the Chinese population in Hong Kong, except for shooting, which was rare.

It is often thought that if a common poison or some other

Table 9. Methods of suicide per 1,000 deaths (1955–9) of the white and the Negro population in the United States (National Office of Vital Statistics). From *Suicide,* by L. I. Dublin.

	White	Negro
Firearms and explosives	391	512
Poisoning	259	130
Hanging and strangulation	213	117
All other methods	136	241

method of suicide were made unavailable, the suicide rate would markedly decline. This is far from certain. In the United States coal gas has been replaced by natural gas which is not toxic, although its inhalation in the absence of oxygen may still be fatal. It is only rarely used for the purpose of suicide. Other methods have taken the place of gassing, which in Great Britain used to head the list of methods (p. 37). The suicide rates of Basle in Switzerland tell the same story. That city had for a long time had a high incidence of suicide, with domestic gas at the head of the list of methods. Its detoxication a few years ago reduced the suicide rate only transiently. After a year it reverted to its previous high level, drowning having taken the place of gassing at the top of the list. A small proportion of suicides are committed with unusual, sometimes bizarre methods. The victims are as a rule people suffering from serious mental illness. There are certain methods, such as jumping from a great height, or lying down on a railway track in the dark, or hanging, which make survival most unlikely. In this country these methods are used only by a minority. Other safeguards against survival are the sealing of doors and windows in case of gassing – this is not uncommon – or the taking of poison in a place where intervention from other people is most unlikely. Many suicides are carried out in circumstances which make intervention and rescue possible. This applies especially to poisoning which is usually done at home where the main safeguard against intervention is timing. The absence of elaborate precautions against survival does not mean that those people expect to be rescued, which they sometimes are. It does, however, illustrate that suicide is not as a rule a rational, carefully planned and executed act. Sometimes the person who is committing suicide contacts other people in the course of the act, either to inform them of his impending death or to request them to rescue him. In addition, *warning* is often given before the event and *notes* are left behind for discovery afterwards.

Warning. Although the majority of suicides come as a shock and surprise to relatives and others, retrospective inquiry frequently reveals that suicidal intentions had been expressed directly or indirectly well in advance of the act. Some psychiatrists reported that sixty to seventy-five per cent of their patients who had committed suicide had given a warning to somebody, though rarely to their doctors. The notion, therefore, that people who threaten suicide do not carry it out is a dangerous error. The implication of the warnings preceding suicidal acts will be discussed in connexion with suicidal attempts.

Notes. Only a minority of people who kill themselves leave a written message behind. Of seventy-three male and forty-four female cases of suicide on which an inquest had been held in a London Coroner's Court during 1953, eighteen and twenty-one respectively left a suicide note, and this was an unusually high proportion. In other groups of cases notes were left by only about fifteen per cent.

There is no evidence that suicide notes are more truthful than other communications made under emotional stress. They usually contain expressions of love or hate. They certainly bear out the importance of aggression against others in the motivation of suicide, especially the revenge motive, and also the desire to be loved, even after death. Of the thirty-nine notes mentioned above, only twenty contained a reference to the motives of the suicide. Suicide notes reflect a remarkable attention to reality present and future. The writers appear to be profoundly interested in what is going to happen after their death, as if they were still going to participate in events. This common feature is in keeping with the contention that man is unable to conceive his individual extinction from the world. Almost invariably, the writers of suicide notes aim at eliciting certain emotional responses from survivors who had been close to them. They often ask for forgiveness. Sometimes society at large is blamed.

A team of psychologists in Los Angeles compared genuine with simulated suicide notes. The latter were obtained from a control group which was carefully matched with the writers of the genuine notes. The experimental subjects were instructed 'to write a suicide note as they might write it were they planning to take their lives'. The verbal contents of those notes were subjected to a careful linguistic analysis. The genuine notes showed more references to persons, things, and spatial relationships than the faked ones. Similar observations were made by Capstick in Wales where the proportion of suicides who left a note behind was the same as in Los Angeles, i.e. fifteen per cent. Relatively more people over sixty left notes behind than in the younger age groups. The notes indicated a striking preoccupation with the things of this world, especially human relations, which contrasted oddly with the wish to die. Whether the writers of suicide notes differ in their attitudes from those who leave no notes behind it is impossible to say. Possibly, they differ from the majority only in being good correspondents. At any rate, the results of the analysis of suicide notes are in keeping with the observation that preoccupation with other people and the urge to influence and to communicate with them are common to most suicidal acts.

*

From time to time two people commit suicide together. This kind of mutual arrangement is called a *suicide pact*. Professor John Cohen of Manchester University studied the records of the fifty-eight couples who killed themselves in England and Wales during 1955–8. They represented 0.6 per cent of the total number of suicides registered during that period. Contrary to common belief, the proportion of unhappy lovers among those who died together was very small. Only five fell into that category. Forty-two of the couples were spouses, most of them sick people. Almost half of them had been childless. Although the notes left behind nearly always state that the decision was evenly shared, the initiative usually comes from one of the two and sometimes a good deal of persuasion has to be used. There are certain typical constellations; the initiator may suffer from depressive illness which has a notoriously depressing effect on those living with him; or both may be old and sick, or two people may have been caught in an extra-marital entanglement. The joint suicide of young lovers whose association is opposed by their parents is extremely rare, at least in this country. In some cases of double suicide the old belief that dying together leads to blissful union after death plays a part in the motivation. Investigation of survivors of suicide pacts sometimes reveals conscious murderous impulses on the part of the initiator. If one of the two partners survives he is liable to be charged with having aided and abetted another person's suicide. This part of the law of suicide has been retained under the new Suicide Act for England and Wales (see p. 72).

Motives and Causes

A great deal has been written about the motives for suicide. Frequently the reasons given by the victims are understandable enough, but they are hardly ever of a nature which would make suicide the only possible action to take. Information about motives is often difficult to obtain as the most important informant can no longer be questioned. The conscious motive is as a rule only the last precipitating factor in a multiplicity of causes. It is nevertheless of interest, if only to dispel misconceptions. Sainsbury attempted to distinguish between contributory and principal causes of suicide in the 390 cases in the records of the Coroner for North London in 1936–8. More than one factor was evident in most cases, but in thirty-eight cases the available information failed to show an adequate cause. Sainsbury grouped the causal factors into five broad categories, shown in Table 10.

Table 10. Causative factors in 390 cases of suicide in North London 1936–8. Modified after P. Sainsbury, *Suicide in London,* 1955.

Factors	Contributory in % of cases	Principal in % of cases
Social factors	60	35
Personal	20	14
Physical illness	29	18
Mental disorder	47	37
Personality abnormal	17	17

These distinctions and their allocation in individual cases are somewhat arbitrary and artificial. Nevertheless, subdivision of causes into the above five categories threw some light on specific problems, e.g. the role of unemployment. During the period under investigation, the suicide rate among the unemployed was much greater than among the corresponding employed population. However, it would be wrong to attribute every suicide of a person out of work to unemployment. This seemed to be justified in only one third of the suicides of unemployed persons. According to Sainsbury, 'it would appear that the unemployed experience in an exaggerated form the disturbance found in all classes at times of economic upheaval. The latter is the common factor causing both suicide and unemployment and so, in some measure, accounting for the association between them.'

An unhappy love affair appeared to have been the principal cause in only fourteen of the 390 suicides investigated retrospectively, and in only two cases was pregnancy in an unmarried female found at the post-mortem investigation. In two cases failed examinations seemed to have been a precipitating cause.

Obviously, the immediate causes and motives of suicide in any sample of cases will depend not only on the social conditions but also on the age of the victims. Physical illness, for instance, or bereavement, are more likely to be precipitating causes in the older age groups, while in the young breakdowns in human relations will be more prominent among the precipitating factors.

In East and Central Africa the most common motives were, in order of frequency, among men physical disease, quarrel with spouse or lover, impotence, mental illness, shame, and bereavement, and among women, physical disease, quarrel with spouse or lover, and infertility. Fifteen per cent of the suicides followed homicidal acts. Not uncommonly suicides were conscious acts of revenge against a person with whom the victim had had a quarrel and who was to appear as responsible for the suicide. The motives for suicide observed in Africa do not differ fundamentally from those found in other parts of the world, although impotence and infertility seem to figure more frequently as main motives there than in the highly developed Western countries.

The study of conscious motives alone, however, cannot elucidate the origin of suicidal tendencies in general and the problem why some people react to certain stresses with suicidal acts. What drives people to killing themselves or, to use a psychological term, what motivates them? Many answers have been given to this question, but only since the end of the last century has it been investigated systematically and with scientific methods. The most important contributions have come from sociologists and psychoanalysts.

Fluctuations of the suicide rates were often manifestly associated with changes in the state of society, such as wars, political upheavals, and economic crises. Here were apparently precise facts which could be related to social factors. It is not surprising that the early sociologists took a lively interest in a subject which lent itself to a statistical approach. In 1878 Thomas Masaryk, then a professor in the university of Prague and later famous as the first president of Czechoslovakia, published a monograph entitled 'Suicide as a social mass phenomenon of modern civilization'. Although his book lacked methodological sophistication, it forestalled some of the later sociological findings. Masaryk, who still believed that suicide did not occur in primitive societies, regarded modern civilization and the decline of religion as responsible for the increase in the suicide rates. There is, it seems, no period of history and no society in which those two factors have not been blamed for this and other types of behaviour which are painful to the community.

E. Durkheim's monograph 'Le Suicide', published in 1897 and translated into English in 1952, is the most important sociological contribution to the problem. Durkheim's main principle was that social facts must be studied as realities external to the individual. Social institutions, such as the family and religious groups, were extra-personal forces. Sociology had to be objective since it dealt with definite realities. The incidence of suicide was one of them. Suicide, although apparently a highly personal act, was explicable only by the state of the society to which the individual belonged. Each society had a collective inclination to suicide expressed in the suicide rate which tended to remain constant as long as the character of the society did not change. This collective inclination of society influenced the individual and could coerce him to kill himself. A certain number of suicides was to be expected in every society. Serious faults in the social structure led to an increase in the suicide rates. The more strongly the individual was integrated with social groups, the smaller was the likelihood of suicide. Therefore suicide was relatively rare among members of big families and of closely knit religious or other social groups.

Durkheim distinguished three types of suicide according to the type of disturbance in the relationship between society and the individual.

Egoistic suicide. Abnormal individualism resulted in a weakening of society's control and reduced the person's immunity against the collective suicidal inclination. This type of suicide was the effect of the individual's lack of concern for the community and inadequate involvement with it.

This category is the least satisfactory of the three. It includes most suicides due to physical and mental illness as well as the suicides of the deprived and the bereaved.

Altruistic suicide. People over whom society had too strict a hold and who had too little individualism could be driven to self-destruction by excessive altruism and sense of duty. This kind of suicide was more common in primitive than in highly developed societies. In this category belonged the old and sick who wanted to relieve society of themselves; the women who followed their husbands into death; the followers or servants who killed themselves on the death of their chiefs. The self-sacrifice of martyrs as well as the *hara-kiri* of Japanese officers were suicides of this type. Altruistic suicide inspired respect and admiration. Captain Oates's self-sacrifice could be classified with this kind of death. The category of altruistic suicide is very small.

Anomic Suicide. If society failed to control and to regulate the behaviour of individuals, a state which Durkheim called *anomie*, suicide became more frequent. The decline of religious beliefs, the excessive relaxation of professional and marital codes were manifestations of anomie. They resulted in disturbances of the collective organization which in turn reduced the individual's immunity against suicidal tendencies. This explained the high incidence of suicide among the divorced.

Egoism and anomie may reinforce each other and lead to mixed types of suicide. Suicide was less frequent in strict and rigid societies than in those which were comparatively liberal and flexible. Therefore, suicides were less common among Roman Catholics than among Protestants.

Durkheim's work has recently been subjected to severe criticism by sociologists. Gibbs and Martin took him to task for having failed to offer a precise definition of 'social integration' and therefore having presented an untestable theory. They set out to make good this omission. They introduced the concept of status, i.e. a category of people with clearly defined roles. Every individual belonged to several statuses, e.g. male – carpenter – married – Negro – parent. The more frequently a combination of statuses in individuals conformed to combinations most common in the population to which they belonged, the higher was its 'status integration' which could be expressed mathematically. There may be status incompatibility with role conflicts, which could be measured. Durkheim's basic theory was reformulated thus: 'The suicide rate of a population varies inversely with the degree of status integration in that population'. The predictions derived from this hypothesis proved on the whole correct, with some exceptions. The authors believed that it accounted for the predominance of male over female suicides and even for seasonal variations. Like most sociologists, they make it a point of honour to use only 'hard' data, such as suicide rates and other measurable factors. But how hard are those data? Gibbs and Martin's work is an attempt at bringing Durkheim up to date.

The study by Henry and Short into the relationship between suicide and homicide to the American business cycle represents yet another attempt at correlating the suicide rates to measurable social factors. Business cycles were shown to change the hierarchical social status of persons and of groups. Loss of status caused frustrations which engendered aggression. The latter tended to be directed either against the self or against others,

according to social conditions. These authors combined sociological with psychopathological theories, but they, too, took the
reliability of the suicide rates for granted.

The most radical attack on the classical sociological theory of
suicide was launched by Jack Douglas, another sociologist.
Durkheim's basic assumptions were rejected as being based on
unreliable data. Sociologists were exhorted to explore the shared
and individual meanings of what appeared to be suicidal acts
taking place in different sociocultural systems. As these meanings
were problematic, the idea of a 'real rate' was a misconception.
Few sociologists will go the whole way with this author, but his
criticism of the suicide rates, whose reliability has been taken for
granted by too many workers in this field, cannot be brushed
under the carpet. In advocating the study of the meaning of
suicidal acts, Douglas allied himself with anthropologists, psychoanalysts and some psychiatrists who have explored the meanings
of suicidal behaviour patterns.

Durkheim put forward his ideas at a time when the study of
human behaviour had hardly begun. His concept of the collective
state of society and its suicidal inclination is only of historical
interest today. While the psychology of the group differs from
that of the individual, it is now recognized that the one cannot be
understood without the other.

The study of the *psychodynamics of suicide*, i.e. of the mental
forces urging the individual to self-destruction, and of the de-
fences against them, has yielded a good deal of insight. While
clinical psychiatrists have concerned themselves with the incidence of suicide in the various mental disorders, psychoanalysts
have examined the suicidal behaviour in the light of their basic
concepts. The psychoanalytic contribution to the problem of
suicide falls into two phases, before and after the postulation of
the death instinct.

In 1910 suicide was discussed at length in Freud's circle. Alfred
Adler, who later dissociated himself from Freud, thought that the
urge to inflict pain and sorrow on the relatives played a significant
part in the motivation of suicide. A constitutional factor, i.e.
the strength of the aggressive drive, was probably also important.

Other speakers made some interesting comments. 'Only he who has given up hope to be loved gives up his life.' 'Nobody kills himself unless he also wants to kill others or at least wishes some other person to die.' 'Nobody kills himself whose death is not wished by another person.' All stressed the importance of the lack of love in the causation of suicide. Freud thought that the study of 'melancholia', i.e. of depressive illness with strong suicidal tendencies, might provide the answer. Several years later he interpreted the urge to self-destruction as an attack against a loved person with whom the individual had identified himself. This theory implied that what appeared to be self-destruction was at least partly an act of homicide, i.e. directed against another person. Even the superficial observer sometimes notes how anger and aggression meant for others can be turned against the self.

At the early stage of psychoanalytic theory aggression was still regarded as a perversion of the sexual drive and as a reaction to frustration. The concept of a primary 'death instinct' was evolved by Freud some years later and first published in 1920 in his essay *Beyond the Pleasure Principle*. He had arrived at the conclusion that, however widely the scope of the drives serving the preservation of the self and of the species was expanded, certain aspects of behaviour could not be fitted into that concept. He assumed that from the beginning of life there was, side by side with the sexual drive, a tendency to disintegration and destruction at work which he called the death instinct. That tendency had passive and active manifestations, acts of aggression belonging to the latter category. Many aspects of human behaviour could be understood as the results of the interplay between sexual drive and death instinct, or, in psychological terms, as the expressions of the interplay of love and hate.

Freud's dualistic theory of drives was not generally accepted even among psychoanalysts. The concept of the death instinct has certain logical difficulties, possibly because it tries to explain too much. It is supposed to account for aggressive behaviour in the accepted sense as well as for the normal and abnormal decline and decay of the organism. This 'biological speculation', as

Freud himself called it, is in need of rethinking and reformulation. Nevertheless, the postulation of a primary aggressive tendency proved a great stimulus for the study of aggressive–destructive behaviour directed against both other persons and the self.

Man Against Himself, for example, was the title of a book by the American psychiatrist Karl A. Menninger, in which every kind of behaviour inimical to health and life was interpreted as the expression of the death instinct directed against the self, of which suicide was thought to be an extreme manifestation. Habitual behaviour resulting in self-injury, e.g. asceticism and martyrdom, alcohol addiction, anti-social behaviour, self-mutilation, purposeful accidents, and some types of mental illness were regarded as chronic or partial suicides.

Other psychoanalysts, who rejected the concept of a death instinct, have expressed the opinion that the human mind is incapable of conceiving death. Man does not wish for extinction but for Nirvana. Suicide is thus seen as an act of self-perpetuation rather than of self-extinction, in which the individual denies the barrier separating life and death. Suicide has been seen as a paradoxical self-assertion through which man achieves a phantasied immortality. Taking one's life is an act of omnipotence because in doing so the person evades natural death. These and other interpretations have been based on the thoughts and phantasies of patients undergoing psychoanalysis. Religious teaching expressed similar views long before psychoanalysis. 'In killing yourself you are taking what only God can give and take away', is the essence of the condemnation of suicide as a cardinal sin.

The study of *suicide phantasies* has thrown some light on the understanding of suicidal acts. In the phantasy, suicide is often a means of forcing others to express their love even after one's death. Tom Sawyer's success in making a whole community profess their love for him and their feeling of guilt for not having shown it while he was alive, is a brilliant description of this kind of phantasy come true.

Conscious motives alone cannot adequately explain suicidal acts because only certain people react in this manner to emotional stress. With very few exceptions, there is no situation causing individuals to commit suicide which would not be tolerated by most other people without the emergence of self-destructive impulses. People who tend to react to stressful situations with suicidal acts are called suicide prone.

Suicide proneness could be based on certain personality features which are part of the individual's innate endowment, or on previous experiences which would tend to make the individual react in this manner, or on both. The former factors were discussed by early psychoanalysts who conceived of the possibility of abnormally strong constitutional aggression directed against the self under certain psychological conditions. The role of previous experiences has received a great deal of attention from psychoanalysts, which is in keeping with their emphasis on environmental factors. Zilboorg found that many people who had committed or attempted suicide had a history of a *broken home in childhood*. This observation has often been confirmed, although the broken home is known to play a part also in the etiology of some other types of abnormal behaviour such as delinquency. The definition of a 'broken home in childhood' varies greatly in the writings of different authors. To some it means lack of at least one parent, while others regard prolonged absence of a parent as sufficient for a home to be so characterized. This means that the homes of most children whose fathers were serving in the military forces during the war have to be included. Some writers speak of a broken home where there is severe parental discord without separation. Another variable is the age within which the loss of a parent constitutes a broken home. The age limit stipulated by some authors is as high as eighteen. The adoption of an agreed definition of what constitutes a broken home would be highly desirable. Only thus could the effect of abnormal family constellations be compared and evaluated. The most recent definition is that of Bruhn who defined a broken home as one characterized by absence or loss of one or both parents, by death or separation due to marital disharmony for periods of six months or more before the patient reached the age of fifteen years. Separation or absence of either parent during periods of war was not included because this kind of forced separation was not as a rule experienced as desertion by the child and did not preclude the maintenance of emotional ties. The above definition considers physical separation only. Other definitions include also severe parental discord, which is often difficult to establish retrospectively. Those who are against the inclusion of the latter criterion have argued that even bad parents and parental discord cause less deprivation than the breaking up of a family by death or separation. Whatever definition of a broken home is adopted, it must be clearly understood that it is only one factor in suicide proneness. Whether or not the liability to suicidal acts becomes manifest will depend on circumstances facing the individual later in life. It is possible, however, that a broken home in childhood may, by creating emotional and social instability, predispose the individual to the kind of crises which tend to result in suicidal acts. This has been suggested by Bruhn's studies in Edinburgh. He compared a group of patients who had attempted suicide with a suitably matched control group of psychiatric out-patients who had not attempted suicide. He found not only that the incidence of a broken home in childhood was significantly higher among the suicidal group, but also that at least one of four factors of social disorganization acted on the individual shortly before or at the time of the suicidal act – household instability through loss of a family member, unemployment, residential mobility, and severe marital disharmony. These observations are in keeping with the general rule that traumatic childhood experiences tend to make the individual unstable and liable to breakdown under emotional stress. Ringel's concept of a specific neurotic development leading to suicide proneness will be discussed later (p. 63).

The lack of a secure relationship to a parent figure in childhood may have lasting consequences for a person's ability to establish relationships with other people. Such individuals are likely to find themselves socially isolated in adult life, and social isolation is one of the most important factors in the causation of suicidal acts. Fortunately, the 'broken home' has no permanent ill-effects, if, as often happens, parent substitutes are found who compensate for the lack or loss of the primary love object.

Durkheim and Freud seem to be worlds apart. No two theories of human behaviour could be more different than the conception of the collective inclination coercing the individual to kill himself and psychoanalytical notions of the origin of suicidal tendencies. Yet the two theories have one important aspect in common; both see the individual's actions as the result of powerful forces over which he has only limited control. Durkheim located those forces in society, Freud in the unconscious. Durkheim's 'collective conscience' supposed to be extra-personal has, in the psychoanalytical theory, its counterpart in the super-ego, i.e. the mental representation of the moral demands. According to Freud the drives are modified and the super-ego is shaped by society. Durkheim and Freud, then, are not quite as incompatible as it would appear. They shared a deterministic view of human behaviour, subjected and subservient to powerful forces of which the person is not fully aware.

It is also worthy of note that a concept similar to the sociological notion of the collective inclination forms part of Jungian psychology. Jung's so-called collective unconscious, too, is a psychic force acting on the individual. The logical difficulties arising from both concepts are considerable. Neither can be easily fitted into a scientific psychology.

Finally, *imitation* has sometimes been regarded as an important factor in suicide. The occasional run of suicides in a family, the fashions in the choice of methods and suicide epidemics favoured such an assumption. However, the urge to imitation alone is unlikely to cause anybody to take his life unless his state of mind predisposes him to such an action and unless there exists a close relationship with the person whose behaviour he adopts. The mental mechanism which leads to this kind of selective imitation has been described as identification. There is no evidence that there is a specific innate predisposition to suicide. There are always special reasons why a member of a family or of some other group should follow another member in committing suicide.

Suicides of whole groups and communities are known to have occurred in times of war and persecution : they were not due to simple imitation but to a collective refusal to survive. So-called suicide fashions are preferences for methods of self-destruction sometimes following the suicide of a well-known person. They are more obvious in non-fatal than in fatal suicidal acts.

5 Suicide and Mental Disorders

Some students of suicide contend that no sane person would kill himself and that, therefore, every individual committing such an act is suffering from a mental disorder, at least at the time of the act. The state of mind in which self-destructive impulses are predominant and active has been described as the suicidal crisis. It has been compared with other abnormal mental states in which consciousness is dominated by powerful drives. This line of reasoning has far-reaching implications. It means that a certain type of abnormal behaviour is by itself a criterion of mental disorder even if no other symptoms are present. Similarly, every person who has committed homicide would have to be regarded as suffering from a mental disorder, possibly with even greater justification, because homicide is rarer than suicide. In analogy to the suicidal crisis, a homicidal crisis would have to be postulated, indeed a crisis for any act which is unusual and can be carried out only if consciousness is dominated by a single drive to the exclusion of other thoughts and emotions. While this argument may be appropriate to certain individual cases, especially where legal responsibility is concerned, it cannot form the basis of a generalization about the relationship between suicidal acts and mental disorder, unless the latter concept is expanded to such a degree that it becomes almost meaningless. This way lies loose thinking and confusion.

At the present state of knowledge, it is reasonable not to accept the suicidal act alone as a criterion of one of the typical mental disorders. Even so, this act has to be regarded as abnormal, in the statistical as well as the behavioural sense, because the vast majority of persons would not react in this way in a similar situation. It can be fitted into the category 'Transient situational disturbances' (No. 307, International Statistical Classification of Diseases).

However, this approach does not dispose of the need to discuss the concept of mental disorder. The clinician regards a person as mentally ill if his condition falls into one of the categories of recognized mental disorders. There are four such broad categories, i.e. the neuroses, which do not as a rule lead to a serious break with reality; the psychoses, which are the more severe disorders often resulting in serious disturbance and break with reality; the abnormal personalities; the mental subnormality or deficiency, i.e. retarded intellectual development. Estimates of the prevalence of these conditions vary from one tenth to one third of the general population. Precise information is difficult to come by because only a proportion of people belonging to these categories seek treatment for their mental abnormalities. Probably only a minority of the neurotics do so, while most of the psychotics sooner or later come under psychiatric treatment. Only a minority of the people belonging to the group of the abnormal personalities are ever seen by a psychiatrist. Of the mentally subnormal, most of the severely handicapped come under medical care, but they do not form the majority of this group.

It is against this background that the relationship between suicide and mental disorders has to be viewed. It has been found that on the average one third of the people who commit suicide have been suffering from a neurosis or psychosis or a severe personality disorder. Suicide seems to be rare among the mentally subnormal.

This does not mean that the remaining two thirds are well balanced personalities. On the contrary, retrospective inquiries have revealed that many of them were emotionally unstable people who might have benefited from psychiatric attention, but who had never been regarded as in need of it. At any rate, the majority of people who commit suicide have not been under psychiatric treatment. This is true for the United Kingdom and probably also for other Western communities. In the rest of the world, where psychiatrists are much scarcer than in the Western countries, the proportion of people committing suicide who have been under psychiatric observation or treatment must be smaller still.

Suicide can occur in most mental disorders. It is rare in organic dementia, i.e. intellectual impairment due to brain lesions and often associated with indifference and apathy. It never occurs in the so-called manic state, a relatively rare condition, the main symptom of which is elation with an exaggerated feeling of happiness.

Many clinicians emphasize the need for distinguishing between psychotic and non-psychotic suicidal acts. This does not mean that the psychotic disorder by itself explains the suicidal act, but only that its motives spring from the symptoms of the psychosis. In depressive illness, for instance, the motives originate from the abnormal affect and the depressive thought contents, as they do in the so-called reactive (non-psychotic) depression which is the most common cause of suicidal acts. The difference lies in the causation of the depression, which in the first case is assumed to be largely endogenous, i.e. due to factors in the organism, in the second case largely exogenous, i.e. due to environmental factors. Motiveless suicide does not exist even in psychotic mental disorder.

Ringel described the 'presuicidal syndrome' as consisting of three symptoms, i.e. the narrowing of mental functions, suppressed aggression and flight into phantasy. The manifestations of the first symptom were inferiority feeling, anxiety, mistrust and resignation; the second symptom provided the predisposition to the turning of aggression against the self; the third consisted of preoccupation with death. All these features are most pronounced in depressive illness.

Depressive illness or melancholia is the mental disorder with the highest suicidal risk. Its main symptom is a severe depression with profound pessimism, a feeling of futility and worthlessness and a tendency to excessive guilt feelings and self-reproach.

Invariably depressed patients wish to die and many, though not all of them, commit or attempt suicide. The intensity of the suicidal urge depends not only on the severity of the depression, but also on the individual's past history. Walton found the likelihood of a suicidal act to be greater among those depressive patients who had a history of a broken home in childhood (see Chapter 3) than among those who grew up in a normal family setting. The etiology of this common mental disorder is still obscure. Only in a minority of cases can the onset of the illness be related to a precipitating event, such as bereavement. In the rest the depression seems to occur without known cause. This is why it has also been called endogenous depression. It usually subsides completely after several months but has a strong tendency to recur. It is an illness of adult life, is not uncommon in late middle age, and may occur also in old age. Its main danger is suicide. Some patients try to persuade their relatives to join them in suicide because they believe that they, too, would be better off dead. They only rarely succeed with adult relatives, but mercy killing of infants is not uncommon. This happens when a depressive illness following childbirth is not diagnosed in time. These cases of infanticide are particularly tragic if the mother, having killed the baby, survives.

These observations illustrate the vital importance of early diagnosis and treatment of depressive illness. This is not always easy because depression is such a common condition and the differentiation of a depressive illness from an excessive reaction to bereavement or disappointment is often difficult, especially for the inexperienced. These so-called reactive depressions, which differ only in degree from normal depressive reactions, may also lead to suicide, but this danger is less than in endogenous depression.

There is no medical man who has never misjudged the risk of suicide in a depressed patient. Psychiatrists have often tried to list the criteria indicative of an impending suicidal act. Here is one such list: (1) Depression with guilt feelings, self-depreciation, and self-accusations, associated with tension and agitation; (2) Severe hypochondriasis, i.e. a tendency to continuous complaining, usually about physical symptoms; (3) Sleeplessness with great concern about it; (4) Fear of losing control, or of hurting others or oneself; (5) Previous suicidal attempt; (6) Suicidal preoccupation and talk; (7) Unsympathetic attitude of the relatives, or life in social isolation; (8) Suicides in the family; (9) History of a broken home before the age of 15; (10) Serious physical illness; (11) Alcohol or drug addiction (the relative frequency of drug addiction among doctors is probably one of the reasons why suicide is more common among them than in a comparable group of the general population); (12) Towards the end of a period of depressive illness, when the depressive mood still persists, but when initiative is returning, the risk of suicide is particularly high; (13) Dreams of catastrophes, falls, and self-destruction are, according to Professor Kielholz of Basle, indicative of increased suicidal risk if they occur in depressed patients; (14) Unemployment and financial difficulties.

Some psychiatrists believe that religious ties make suicide in depressive illness less likely. Although it is true that suicides are in general less common among the devout than among the non-religious, it would be unwise to rely on this rule in the assessment of the suicidal risk in depressive illness. Patients suffering from this mental disorder commonly complain about having lost their faith, which adds to their guilt feelings and may increase the danger of suicide.

Schizophrenics sometimes commit suicide, especially in the early stages of the illness when they may experience a sinister feeling of impending catastrophe. Their outward behaviour may still be quite normal. Some of the unexpected and mysterious suicides of young people are attributable to this condition, which in a proportion of cases is a disabling and chronic mental illness with hallucinations and delusions. Occasionally, schizophrenics kill themselves under the influence of voices ordering them to do so, or to escape persecutions, but this is rare.

Most *abnormal personalities* have a high suicide proneness. This is particularly true of the so-called hysterical personality which tends to react to frustration with physical symptoms or transient abnormal mental states such as memory loss. These people have an insatiable urge for love and attention from their fellow-men and sometimes they consciously exploit the appeal effect of the suicidal act for this purpose. It would, however, be a mistake to regard the majority of suicidal acts as hysterical because they have an appeal effect. Their impact on other people only explains why hysterical personalities should so often be tempted to risk their lives in that way.

Ringel regards suicide proneness as the result of a chronic neurotic personality development which may originate either from a broken home or from other anomalies of human relationships in childhood. Early inhibition, discouragement and defective ego-development were characteristic features, while typical neurotic symptoms were as a rule absent. These individuals tended to be subject to disappointments and failures which were often self-inflicted. This neurotic development has much in common with the psychoanalytical concept of the character neurosis and in particular with the 'masochistic personality' in which self-damaging tendencies appear to influence the individual's development and his destiny. Ringel's concept of the neurotic development arising from certain traumatic childhood experiences complements the emphasis on the broken home in Anglo-American literature. It fills in the gap between the traumatic experience and the emergence of the suicidal behaviour pattern. The real test of this clinical concept will be its value for the prediction of suicidal acts in individuals.

Anti-social psychopaths, i.e. individuals who show abnormally aggressive and irresponsible conduct, also have an excessive suicide proneness. They find it difficult to cope with their very strong aggressive impulses which they sometimes turn against themselves. In such individuals the tendency to acts of violence against others and to violent self-injury with suicidal intent often coexist. This accounts partly for the relatively high incidence of suicidal acts in the prison population.

Another group of abnormal personalities with an excessive suicide proneness are alcoholics. Habitual alcohol abuse and other addictions have been regarded as forms of chronic suicide. According to this view they are substitutes for the typical suicidal acts and serve the desire to escape from reality. If this was the only relationship between addictions and suicides, the latter ought to be infrequent among addicts. However, the opposite holds true. There is a positive correlation between the amount of alcohol consumed in a community and its suicide rate. The reasons for this are manifold. People who are prone to depressive moods, and therefore to suicide, tend to resort to alcohol for its temporary stimulating action. Far from being a reliable anti-depressant, alcohol has in many cases a depressing effect. It also tends to reduce inhibitions and self-control, thus releasing suicidal and other aggressive impulses. This is why so many people take alcohol before committing or attempting suicide even if they are not in the habit of drinking to excess.

The incidence of suicide in mental hospitals is higher than in the general population, for two reasons. Firstly, the suicide proneness of the mentally ill is well above average and a considerable proportion of psychiatric patients have suicidal thoughts and impulses at times or for long periods. Secondly, it would be quite impossible to observe all hospital patients so closely and continuously that suicidal acts would be impossible. This kind of observation can be provided only for a very small number of acutely suicidal patients at a time. Nevertheless, the hospital environment and treatment reduce the risk of suicide among the mentally ill. A survey of the number of suicides among patients resident in the mental hospitals of England and Wales between 1920 and 1947 revealed that the rates per 100,000 were about four to five times that of the general population. This means, in terms of the present-day suicide rate of eleven for the whole country, forty-four to fifty-five suicides per 100,000 psychiatric hospital patients, i.e. about one suicide per year in a hospital of 2,000 patients, which is not excessive. The number of patients resident in psychiatric hospitals including those for the subnormals was 193,000 in 1961.

The Attitudes of Society to Suicide

Attitudes to suicide are closely linked with ideologies of death. This accounts for the similarities and the differences between the reactions of various societies to suicide. In most cultures and in most periods of history the attitude to suicide has had something in common with that to homicide: both are dreaded and forbidden but there are exceptional circumstances in which they are allowed. Homicide is permitted in self-defence and in war. Suicide, too, is felt by society to be permissible under certain conditions.

In a discussion of the attitudes of various societies to suicide it might be illuminating to start with so-called primitive societies. The American anthropologist Paul Bohannan and his associates studied attitudes to suicide in six African tribes living in Nigeria, Uganda, and Kenya. Among all of them suicide was considered evil. Physical contact with the body or the surroundings of a suicide were feared to have disastrous effects, one of which was suicide among his kin. Various measures were taken to prevent those consequences; in one of the tribes the body had to be removed by a person unrelated to the dead man and his kin, the service being repaid by the gift of a bull. In another tribe a sheep had to be killed to pacify the spirit of the suicide. His hut had to be pulled down or thoroughly purified according to certain rituals. In several East African tribes the tree on which a person had hanged himself had to be felled and burnt. Suicide was regarded as the expression of the wrath of the ancestors who had to be placated by sacrifices. The body was buried without the usual rituals. Suicide was dreaded in the community and a threat of suicide was sometimes used to exert pressure on the family. In some tribes suicide was believed to be due to witchcraft, and the place where it had happened was believed to be a haunt of evil spirits. Similar fears are not uncommon in Europe even today.

Physical illness sometimes led to suicide.

A man or woman who is ill is to a large extent outside the society, unable to take part in communal activity. When illness first attacks an individual, the support of the community is felt by him or her in the efforts that are made to cure the disease. If all remedies fail, the attitude changes; some people may even attribute the affliction to a supernatural punishment for evil doing. The isolation engendered by this situation may well lead to suicide. (Bohannan)

The attitude to the chronic invalid in Western society is very similar, especially if he becomes a burden to his family.

Attitudes and reactions to suicide among primitive Asian communities are similar to those in Africa. Malinowski made a study of suicide among the Trobriand islanders in the Melanesian archipelago. There were two recognized methods: jumping off the top of a palm tree and taking poison. Motivations were complex and included self-punishment, revenge, and rehabilitation in the eyes of the community. Violation of taboos and loss of status were common motives. Malinowski reported two cases of suicide by young people who had transgressed against the sexual prohibitions of their clans. Both of them put on festive attire and ornamentation before jumping off the top of the palm tree. Loss of status played a part in suttee, the more or less voluntary suicide of the widow in India and other parts of the Far East where widowhood used to bring with it special degradation. The desire for union in death with the deceased husband was the most important conscious motive for this kind of suicide. Suttee is now a criminal offence.

The most recent study of attitudes towards suicide in a primitive community is that carried out in Tikopia by Raymond Firth in 1952. Tikopia is a small island in the Western Pacific with a population of 2,000. Their attitude toward suicide is one of mild disapprobation. Christianity has not had much influence on the islanders' pagan ideology. The gods receive the souls of the dead but not of those who hang themselves. Their souls wander about until their ancestral spirits have found them. The spirits do not object if a man commits suicide by going off to sea in a canoe, or a woman by swimming out to sea. These methods of suicide are admired. The Christian Tikopians believe that the soul of a suicide does not go to Paradise but to Satan.

Death as a means of self-sacrifice and self-purification is sometimes sought by religious fanatics in the East and the tombs of some of these are sacred shrines. Certain Buddhist sects encourage this kind of suicide in the cause of their religion. A press report of 11 August 1963 illustrates this.

Last week for the second time a Buddhist monk in South Vietnam poured petrol over himself and lit it. This violent and horrible death, like the first one in June, was designed to draw attention to the alleged discrimination of the eight million Buddhists in South Vietnam by the 1,250,000 Roman Catholics.

During the following weeks several more suicides of this type occurred. By ignoring them the South Vietnamese Government no doubt hastened its own downfall.

Gandhi's fasts presented the most persistent use of the threat of suicide for political purposes. By taking it seriously, the British administration prevented a great deal of bloodshed. It has been said that it surrendered to blackmail, but everybody faced with a serious threat of suicide has to yield to a certain degree, just as much as a man threatened with a gun, unless he wants to be killed.

The Japanese custom of *hara-kiri*, i.e. ritual self-disembowelling, is an example of the heroic and ceremonial suicide, which used to be reserved for the nobility and the military caste. Compulsory *hara-kiri* ordained by the feudal chief was made illegal in 1868. Voluntary *hara-kiri* as expiation for defeat or as self-sacrifice was highly praised. It is not practised in Japan today: the *hara-kiri* of the writer Mishima Yukio in 1970 was an exception. The methods used by the large number of people who kill themselves in that country are similar to those employed elsewhere. This was probably always the case, but the rare ceremonial suicides were so much in the public eye that the other less heroic ones were hardly mentioned.

Carstairs studied the relationship between attitudes to death and to suicide in an Indian community. He observed a rare type of behaviour in which a religious fanatic made himself go into a state of detachment from reality which culminated in his being buried alive at his own request, in a religious ceremony. For the Hindu death is not final but one incident in a long series of existences. There are timely and untimely deaths, suicide usually belonging to the latter category, and leading to an earth-bound ghostly after-life. In India, as elsewhere, attitudes to death and suicide represent 'attempts to allay the anxieties invariably occasioned by the threat of death'. Since the threat of death is universal, basic attitudes to suicide are similar all over the world, notwithstanding the differences in their manifestations due to different cultural backgrounds.

Contrary to Buddhism and Brahminism, which tolerate or even encourage suicide under certain conditions, Islam condemns it unconditionally. While neither the Old nor the New Testament forbids suicide explicitly, the Koran does so on several occasions. It even declares suicide a much graver crime than homicide. The Old Testament mentions only four cases of suicide, the best known being those of Samson and King Saul, both of whom killed themselves to avoid death by the enemy. Samson, in bringing about his own death, also revenged himself on his adversaries by destroying them in the same act. It has been argued that in biblical times suicide was so rare that no explicit prohibition was called for.

In ancient Greece and in Rome attitudes to suicide varied between condemnation and admiration. Some philosophers recommended suicide as the perfect way of gaining freedom from suffering. Others, among whom were Pythagoras and Plato, strongly disapproved of it for reasons similar to those later advanced by Christianity.

The Christian church in the middle ages condemned suicide as a form of murder. St Augustine denounced it as a crime under all circumstances. At the Council of Arles, in A.D. 452, it was declared to be an act inspired by diabolical possession and a century later it was ordained that the body of the suicide be refused a Christian burial. In some countries the property of the suicide was confiscated, a stake was driven through the body and it was buried at the crossroads, a custom which goes back to pre-Christian times. The last suicide thus treated in England was a man called Griffiths who was buried in London at the crossroads formed by Eaton Street, Grosvenor Place, and King's Road in 1823. There is plenty of evidence that the acts of violence and indignity perpetrated against the dead body were at least partly due to fears of evil spirits released by the suicide; the fears were of the same kind as those which underlie similar actions in Africa and elsewhere. This is not surprising, because it is in his attitudes towards death that modern man has emancipated himself least from the superstitions of his forebears.

The attitude of the Church to suicide has remained one of condemnation, but the sanctions applied in cases of death through suicide are not equally severe in all Christian denominations. The funeral rites accorded to the suicide differ more or less from those commonly due to Christians who have died a natural death. While Judaism and the two other great religions derived from it disapprove of suicide unconditionally, public opinion expressed in Europe and North America has been as ambivalent and divided as in ancient Greece and Rome. There were apologists for suicide even among the clergy. The most famous was John Donne, the Dean of St Paul's, whose posthumous book entitled *Biothanatos* was published in 1644, thirteen years after his death. He denied that suicide was invariably sinful and pleaded for charity and understanding. David Hume, in his 'Essay on Suicide' proclaimed man's right to dispose of his own life and pointed out that nowhere in the Scriptures was suicide expressly prohibited. In France, Montaigne, Voltaire, and Rousseau expressed similar views.

Kant, on the other hand, regarded suicide as an offence against the categorical imperative and the supreme principles of duty which to him was a universal law of nature. William James, the great American psychologist, who was himself a sufferer from depressions with suicidal thoughts, arrived at a similar conclusion and regarded religious faith as the most powerful safeguard against suicide.

Today the public attitude towards suicide is less dogmatic than it used to be in the past, although it was never wholly condemnatory. In their readiness to compromise about homicide, the great religions have truly reflected the sentiments of man throughout the ages. Their uncompromising condemnation of suicide has been somewhat out of keeping with those sentiments. Recently, though, there has been a softening of the attitude to suicide in some quarters of religious leadership in this country. Their part in the change in the English law of suicide is discussed below.

Suicide and the Common Law. The fact that a certain type of misconduct is condemned as sin by religion does not necessarily make it a crime against the law of the land. Adultery is an example of such an offence against the moral code laid down by religion. The anti-suicide laws in ancient Rome and in medieval Europe have a complex history. It is doubtful whether religious considerations alone can account for them. Some historians have connected them with the numerous suicides among slaves which resulted in serious loss of property. The increasing severity of the sanctions of the medieval Church has been related to the need to put a stop to religious self-sacrifice and to the frequent suicides of young females following rape, which was all too common in those war-ridden times. The Council of Nîmes, 1184, made the condemnation of suicide part of the Canon Law. It may have been a crime under the law of England as early as the tenth century, no doubt under the influence of religious views, although Holdsworth puts the date from which suicide was quite clearly a crime as late as 1485. Under certain conditions suicide was punishable even under the Roman Law. In Rome a person accused or convicted of a capital crime could save his estate for his heirs by killing himself and thus evading the implementation of judgement. To obviate this, legislation was introduced which made suicide in those circumstances a confession of the crime carrying with it confiscation of property. Later suicide alone resulted in forfeiture of property under the Roman law.

In England suicide was equated with murder as a criminal offence (*felo de se*) and attempted suicide a misdemeanour from about 1554, following the suicide of Mr Justice Hales, until 1961. The suicide legislation in other European countries used to be the same as in England until the end of the eighteenth and the early part of the nineteenth century. The first country to repeal this law was France in 1790, followed by Prussia six years later and by Austria only in 1850. Suicide is still punishable by law in some countries which were once under British sovereignty. In Scotland suicide has not by itself been an offence against the law for many years although it can lead to the charge of a breach of the peace. This charge is only brought on the rare occasions on which the suicidal act involves a serious public nuisance.

Like many laws which are out of keeping with public sentiment, the English law of suicide was not implemented consistently. In the large majority of suicides the coroners gave a verdict that the balance of mind was disturbed, which avoided the pronouncement of a felony. However, the number of prosecutions for attempted suicide was far from negligible. During the years 1946–55 the number of suicidal attempts known to the police in England and Wales was 44,956, which can have been only a fraction of the true incidence. 5,794 were brought to trial. All but 347 were found guilty. 308 were sentenced to terms of imprisonment without the option of a fine, the rest were put on probation or fined. The law used to be implemented capriciously and caused much hardship. As late as 1955 a sentence of two years' imprisonment was imposed on a man for trying to commit suicide in prison, a sentence which was varied on appeal to the Lord Chief Justice, who substituted for it a nominal sentence of one month's imprisonment.

There was no evidence that the threat of prosecution had a deterrent effect. The pressure for the repeal of the suicide law came mainly from the medical profession, but also from a strong body of magistrates and lastly from the clergy. It seems odd that only a few years ago in some parts of this country a policeman used to sit at the bedside of unconscious patients in hospital until they were fit to be interviewed.

In 1959 the then Archbishop of Canterbury set up a committee under the chairmanship of J. T. Christie to examine whether attempted suicide should continue to be punishable by law. One of the members of the committee was Dr Doris Odlum who had campaigned against the suicide law for many years and was the chairman of a joint committee of the British Medical Association and the Magistrates' Association, both of which had long been in favour of repeal. The Committee reported a year later and published its proceedings and its recommendations. The latter were quite unambiguous. Attempted suicide should cease to be a crime and suicide should no longer be a felony. There should be an alternative burial service for use in certain cases of suicide, i.e. those which were manifestly 'selfish'. Finally the committee recommended that the clergy should take a special pastoral interest in those tempted to commit suicide and in those who attempted it.

The Suicide Act 1961 brought the campaign for a change of the law to a successful conclusion. It abrogated the law whereby it was a crime for a person to commit suicide. In consequence, attempted suicide ceased to be a misdemeanour. The Act made it a criminal offence to aid, abet, counsel, or procure the suicide of another person, thus allaying the fears of those who thought that the repeal of the old law would encourage suicide pacts.

Shortly after the passing of the Suicide Act the Ministry of Health in London issued a memorandum advising all doctors and authorities concerned that attempted suicide was to be regarded as a medical and social problem and that every such case ought to be seen by a psychiatrist. This attitude to suicide is much more in keeping with present-day knowledge and sentiment than the purely moralistic and punitive reaction expressed in the old law.

The relationship between *life insurance and suicide* has sometimes given rise to difficult legal and financial problems. To some people the idea that their suicide will benefit their families financially has a peculiar attraction, while others may feel less hesitant to commit suicide if they know their families are insured against destitution. Exceptional cases like that of the young lawyer who in 1960 killed himself and thirty-four passengers by blowing up the plane in which he was flying over North Carolina have caused some anxiety among the travelling public. He had shortly before his death taken out a life and accident insurance of about $900,000. In this case the incriminating evidence led the insurance companies to withhold payment of benefits on the ground that their client had committed suicide within the two years' contestable period. An appeal against that decision resulted in a settlement of 10 to 15 per cent of the amount involved. Whenever an apparently inexplicable air crash occurs, the possibility of some such cause is thought of, but it must be extremely remote, judging from the observations of the insurance companies. It is true that, according to Dublin, the mortality from suicide among the policy holders with large amounts of insurance is higher than in a comparable group of the general population, but this is in keeping with the higher suicide risk among the upper socioeconomic classes.

Most insurance companies regard suicide as a natural risk and insist only on a clause providing for the return of the premium without interest in the event of the policy holder committing suicide within two years after taking out the insurance. This clause is meant to serve as a safeguard against the person who may think of taking out a life insurance with the intention of committing suicide once the contract becomes valid. The onus of proof that death was due to suicide rests with the insurance company. However, if suicide is due to mental disorder the presumption is, according to Dublin, always in favour of death from natural causes, suicide being regarded as a symptom of the illness. This means that, in America at least, the two years' suicide clause does not apply to those cases. Despite some striking cases, suicide is not now a serious financial problem to the life-insurance companies of the United States, and there is no evidence that the position is different in this country. There is no suicide rush after the elapse of the contestable period of two years.

Part II

Attempted Suicide

The Suicidal Attempt as a Behaviour Pattern, and its Definition

The conventional notion of a genuine suicidal act is something like this: 'A person, having decided to end his life, or acting on a sudden impulse to do so, kills himself, having chosen the most effective method available and having made sure that nobody interferes. When he is dead he is said to have succeeded and the act is often called a successful suicidal attempt. If he survives he is said to have failed and the act is called an unsuccessful suicidal attempt. Death is the only purpose of this act and therefore the only criterion of success. Failure may be due to any of the following causes: the sense of purpose may not have been strong enough; or the act may have been undertaken half-heartedly because it was not quite genuine; the subject was ignorant of the limitations of the method; or he was lacking in judgement and determination through mental illness.' Judging by those standards only a minority of fatal and very few non-fatal suicidal acts would pass muster, as both serious and genuine. The rest have to be dismissed as poor efforts some of which succeeded by chance rather than design. Obviously, this approach cannot do justice to a very common and varied behaviour pattern.

If a visiting scholar from one of the inhabited planets came to earth to study the human species, he would sooner or later notice that some humans sometimes commit acts of self-injury. He would observe that occasionally this self-damaging behaviour causes the person's death, but it would hardly occur to him that this relatively rare outcome is the main purpose of that behaviour.

Having been taught that careful observation of as many subjects as possible is essential before one draws conclusions about the purpose of a certain type of behaviour, and having also learned that the subjects' explanations can be highly misleading, he would watch as many such acts as possible, together with their antecedents and consequences, without preconceived ideas, over a fairly long period. His report on his observations would read like this: 'There are some humans who damage themselves more or less badly and in about one in eight cases the damage is so severe that they die. Whatever the outcome, most of them give a hint or a clear warning to one or several of their fellow humans well before the act, telling them that they are thinking of killing themselves. Those fellow humans may or may not take notice of this warning. But once a person is found to have committed an act of self-damage there is invariably a great commotion among the other humans. They clearly show that they wish the act had never been committed. They do everything to keep him alive and to undo the damage that he did to himself. They go even further than this. While they usually do not show much concern about and sympathy with the suffering of fellow humans, an act of self-injury by one of themselves seems to make them take a profound and most active interest in him, at least for a time. They behave as if they had to help him and to put him on his feet. As a result, his situation is transiently or permanently transformed for the better. These helpful reactions are particularly marked in the members of his family group, but the larger community to which the human belongs also takes part.

'If one looked at the acts of self-damage alone one would be led to believe that self-destruction is their only purpose. But if one considers certain antecedents and the consequences of these acts, this simple explanation cannot be sustained. Why should these humans so often warn others of their intention to damage themselves, especially as they must know that this kind of behaviour is dreaded in their family group and the community? They must also know that, once they have injured themselves, everybody will be upset and will want to help them, and if they should die, many other humans will feel they ought to have helped them. It looks as if their peculiar behaviour cannot be derived from one single tendency but is probably due to a combination of at least two tendencies, one of which might be the urge to self-damage and possibly self-destruction, the other the urge to make other humans show concern and love and act accordingly. There are other peculiar features in the self-damaging behaviour of humans, but these seem the most important.'

The purpose of this fictitious report from unprejudiced space is to bring home the need for a new and very careful look at suicidal behaviour. The most striking difference between the conventional view of suicidal acts and that of the unprejudiced observer lies in his emphasis on the reactions of the environment. The possibility of such reactions and their occasional exploitation has long been known, but this is believed to occur only in suicidal attempts regarded as non-genuine. All genuine suicidal acts are understood to aim at death alone. It is this notion which the uncommitted observer refuses to accept. On what facts does he base his challenge?

DEFINING ATTEMPTED SUICIDE

The death of a person by suicide gives rise to a great number of questions all of which are concerned with facts and events preceding the act. This is why all suicide research has been retrospective, like any other post-mortem investigation. As such, it has considerable limitations because the chief source of information is no longer available. Only in a minority of cases can records such as hospital case notes be obtained which are of help in the reconstruction of the antecedents. Usually one has to rely on whatever information the victim left behind and on hearsay. Attempted suicides have often been used for research into the causes and motives of suicide, the assumption being that they are minor suicides. Therefore, investigations of suicidal attempts were purely retrospective and concerned with the same problems as those of suicide. This line of inquiry is perfectly legitimate and necessary, but until recently research workers ignored the obvious difference between suicides and attempted suicides, i.e. that the former are all dead while the latter are alive. At least, they have survived the suicidal act.

Studies into the fate of people who attempt suicide have been carried out only during the last two decades. They are the follow-up investigations undertaken by Dahlgren at Malmö, by Pierre B. Schneider at Lausanne and by Stengel and his associates at London. These studies have thrown light on how many members of large groups of people who had attempted suicide finally killed themselves.

The London team also investigated the social significance and effects of suicidal attempts. They started from the hypothesis that those who attempted and those who committed suicide consti-tuted two different groups or 'populations'. They set themselves the task of investigating the following questions: 'What is the relationship between the two populations: those who commit suicide and those who attempt suicide? How many kill themselves later, and what makes them liable to do so? How does the suicidal attempt affect the patient's mental state? If suicide was motivated by a crisis in human relations, were those modified by the suicidal attempt, and if so, how? What is the effect of the suicidal attempt on the patient's group and what are their reactions to it? Sociologists have stated that suicide is due to social disintegration and isolation. Do these factors hold good for the suicidal attempt, and, if so, are they influenced by it? Some of these questions are of immediate practical interest for the clinician. The study of others might help us to understand the function of the suicidal attempt in our society.' (Stengel)

Research carried out since these questions were first posed in 1952 makes it possible to answer some of them tentatively today. The hypothesis that those who attempted and those who com-mitted suicide constituted two different groups or 'populations' was confirmed when unselected samples of both were compared statistically (p. 91). The formulation concerning the two popula-tions has nevertheless given rise to serious misunderstandings. It has in fact been borrowed from epidemiology, which is the study of disease phenomena in groups or 'populations' which may over-lap. It was, for instance, perfectly legitimate at the time when tuberculosis was a killing disease to divide patients into two populations, i.e. those who died from the disease and those who recovered, which did not mean that only the former were genuine cases; this division led to a better understanding of the various factors on which the outcome of the disease depended, and it also focused attention on the problems of the survivors. Or, to give an example relevant to the suicide problem, it has been stated, quite correctly, that patients suffering from depressive illness and persons committing suicidal acts present two different populations (Sainsbury). This simply states, in the language of epidemiology, the well-known truth that not everybody who commits a suicidal act is suffering from depressive illness, nor vice versa. However, many members of the former group, or population, belong also to the latter. For the investigation of certain problems it may be essential to study those two groups separately, as was done by Walton (p. 61) who showed that they differed with regard to the history of a broken home.

Unfamiliarity with this use of the term 'population', and the preference for the simple over the complex proposition, have led to the misconception that those two 'populations' were meant to consist of altogether different and mutually exclusive types of individuals. Some students of suicide readily, though erroneously, accepted this notion, while others, quite rightly, contested it, although it had never been put forward by the present author. That those who committed and those who attempted suicide differed statistically by age and sex had first been noted in a small sample by S. Peller, one of the pioneers of epidemiology, in 1932.

The *definition* of what constitutes a suicidal attempt is far from simple. If a person is taken to hospital in a drowsy or comatose state, having left a suicide note behind, and if he admits that he wanted to take his life, there is no problem about the nature of his action. However, if another person, having been admitted in a similar condition denies suicidal intentions and contends that he took an overdose by mistake, or because he wanted to have a good sleep, is he to be regarded as a suicidal attempt? Or if a teenager, after a row with her boy-friend, swallows a boxful of her mother's sleeping pills in his presence, with the obvious intention of impressing him, is she to be classed as a suicidal attempt? Or was this only a demonstrative suicidal gesture or threat? In practice the layman's answer to this question will depend on the effect of the pills and on the reactions of the environment. If the girl falls into a coma, has to be rushed into hospital and survives, the incident will be called a suicidal attempt. If she dies it will be a case of suicide. But if the boy-friend has the presence of mind to make her drink a tumbler of concentrated salt water immediately after she has swallowed the tablets and thus to make her vomit them before they have been absorbed, the whole episode may be over in a few minutes and be dismissed as just another lovers' tiff. However, it will be remembered if she should repeat the act at some later date, perhaps with a less harmless outcome. This example illustrates that the degree of damage and even the outcome of a suicidal act may depend on outside intervention, irrespective of the seriousness of the suicidal intent.

Many people deny suicidal intention after an act of self-damage, because they feel ashamed and guilty. They may not want to tell the truth, or their intention may have been confused at the time. It is generally believed that most if not all people who commit suicidal acts are clearly determined to die. The study of attempted suicides does not bear this out. Many suicidal attempts and quite a few suicides are carried out in the mood 'I don't care whether I live or die', rather than with a clear and unambiguous determination to end life. A person who denies, after what seems an obvious suicidal attempt, that he *really* wanted to kill himself, may be telling the truth. Most people, in committing a suicidal act, are just as muddled as they are whenever they do anything of importance under emotional stress. Carefully planned suicidal acts are as rare as carefully planned acts of homicide. Many are carried out on sudden impulse, although suicidal thoughts were usually present before. At any rate, the person concerned cannot be the sole guide to the interpretation of his conduct. Doctors and others who have to make up their minds about acts of self-damage have to adopt a definition like this: '*A suicidal act is any deliberate act of self-damage which the person committing the act could not be sure to survive.*' Clinicians as well as lay persons ought to regard all cases of potentially dangerous self-poisoning or self-inflicted injury as suicidal acts whatever the victim's explanation, unless there is clear evidence to the contrary. 'Potentially dangerous' means in this context: believed by the 'attempter' possibly to endanger life. For instance, if a person who is ignorant of the effects of drugs takes double or three times the prescribed dose, this might have to be regarded as a suicidal attempt because in taking that overdose the person took a risk which may have proved fatal. However, if a doctor or a nurse took the same dose, the act may not be regarded as a suicidal attempt but only as a gesture. The same applies to injuries with cutting instruments, and to other means of self-damage. To draw an example from literature, the blind Gloucester's jump in *King Lear* from what he thought to be the cliffs of Dover was subjectively a serious suicidal attempt, but in reality quite harmless.

Was it a serious suicidal attempt? This is a question immediately asked in every case by everybody who gets to know about the attempt. The question may have various meanings. It may refer to the chances of survival while the outcome is still in the balance. As the term suicidal attempt is in this book used only for nonfatal suicidal acts, this version of the question need not be discussed here.

There is a good deal of confusion about the criteria of the seriousness of a suicidal attempt, even among experts. Should the degree of self-inflicted damage, i.e. the depth of the coma, the amount of blood lost, in short, the degree of the danger to life, be the sole yardstick? If so, a carefully planned act of self-destruction which was prevented from taking effect by timely intervention may have to be classed as harmless.

Some writers call an attempt serious if it caused severe physical dysfunction or if the suicidal intention was serious. But, there is another aspect which has to be taken into account, i.e. the possibility of intervention from the environment. A lethal dose of a narcotic taken with genuine intent in a situation in which immediate counter-measures can be instituted may not seriously endanger life. On the other hand, a relatively small overdose taken half-heartedly by a person in poor health in a situation where help is not available may be fatal. If danger to life is to be the criterion of the seriousness of a suicidal act, the following aspects, which can be recorded with the help of rating scales, have to be taken into account. (1) The risk taken, i.e the degree of danger to life the person could subjectively have believed he would incur. This factor is closely related to the conscious suicidal intent if there was any. (2) The hazard actually incurred. This can be assessed only by experts. Often there is a marked discrepancy between (1) and (2). If the latter was nil or slight, the suicidal act is often dismissed as non-genuine or negligible, while (1) may in fact have been considerable. Doctors often make the mistake of taking it for granted that their patients' and their own knowledge of the effects of drugs do not differ. (3) The damage suffered, e.g. degree and duration of disturbance of consciousness and of other effects of the poison, degree of the injury, etc., and (4) the social constellation at the time of the act, i.e. the chances of intervention and rescue as they could have been perceived by the person committing the act. The majority of the fatal or almost fatal suicidal acts have a high rating in at least two of those three criteria. To give an example : a suicidal attempt by a person who takes a heavy overdose of sleeping tablets with strong suicidal intention in his home and is found unconscious by a member of his family will not rank as highly on the dangerousness or 'lethality' scale as a similar act undertaken in a hotel room or on a lonely moor. From this point of view, only a minority of suicidal acts, fatal and non-fatal, qualify for top scores. Ettlinger and Flordh, two Swedish investigators, found that of 500 attempted suicides only four per cent could be regarded as well planned, but only seven per cent were more or less harmless.

The classification of the vast number of non-fatal potentially suicidal acts has exercised the minds of many workers ever since attempted suicide has received special attention. The acts subsumed under this term not only differ greatly in dangerousness but also in the degree and clarity of conscious suicidal intention.

Should they all be classed as attempted suicides even if the hazard incurred and the physical damage inflicted were negligible? Some writers distinguish between (a) 'suicidal gestures' in which the communicative and the manipulative purpose of the act is prominent and self-destructive intention apparently absent, (b) ambivalent attempts in which the person was aware of his indecision and apparently could not make up his mind whether he wanted to die or to live, and (c) the determined deliberate suicidal attempt which was intended and could be expected to be fatal by both the attempter and by others. There is also the problem of drawing a line between a suicidal gesture and the pretence of such a behaviour pattern undertaken with due safeguards and without any risk. Shneidman classifies non-fatal suicidal acts according to the person's statements about his intentions to bring about his death as follows: intentioned, subintentioned, unintentioned and contra-intentioned, the last category referring to those only pretending and having made sure of survival. It can be argued that the latter, the contra-intentioned group, should be excluded from this grouping, as the person takes no risk. They are nevertheless of interest to the student of suicidal behaviour because they give rise to the question why some people choose this particular type of malingering and attention-seeking. It could also be questioned whether the 'unintentioned' group, i.e. the gestures, should be included if the assessors are satisfied that self-destructive intentions were absent.

This approach which uses professed or apparent intention rather than overt behaviour as criterion is full of pitfalls which have already been referred to in this chapter. It also has far-reaching consequences for statistics and prevention. This is illustrated by the following case, reported in the *Guardian* in the autumn of 1968. As the names mentioned in the newspaper report are not relevant for this presentation they are not reproduced here.

Prisoner died in 'suicide gesture'

A man found dead in his cell at W. Prison, three weeks ago made a suicide gesture rather than a deliberate attempt on his life, and accidentally killed himself, the deputy Coroner, Mr G. A. E., said yesterday. A verdict of misadventure was recorded on G.G.R., serving a two-year sentence for theft.

Dr B., pathologist, said R. had died from vagal inhibition, pressure on the vagal nerve in the neck causing the heart to stop.* He had been on the floor, near a broken table, with prison uniform straps round his neck.

Dr W.S., senior medical officer at the prison, said R. was given to histrionic displays to draw attention to himself. In July he inflicted a wound on his wrist and said it was a suicide attempt. The doctor thought this a 'gesture to gain admission to hospital' not a 'genuine suicide attempt'.

It was a misjudgement to classify the first act of self-injury as a purely manipulative gesture, i.e. as 'unintentioned or contraintentioned' in spite of the man's assertion to the contrary. The warning was ignored. The doctor obviously saw only the appeal component of the motivations and dismissed the self-destructive tendency as non-existent. It can be assumed that this view was conveyed to the prison staff who were not alerted to the risk of suicide. At any rate, the man was left with the means of hanging himself. At the inquest the doctor stuck to his guns and the case was duly registered as an accident, the onus being put squarely on the victim and on Providence. Everybody else who might otherwise have been involved and who could have prevented this death, if only they had heeded the warning, i.e. the medical officer and the prison administration, was cleared. Public opinion was reassured. One case was lost to the suicide statistics. Society's collusion in evading a sense of guilt for ignoring the appeal for help was all too obvious. Considering the importance of precedent in legal matters, one can safely assume that more such 'accidents' will occur in prisons in this country unless the people who are responsible for the care of the prison population, and also H M. Coroners, are better informed about the complexity of motivations of suicidal acts. This kind of occurrence shows the need for an operational definition of suicidal, attempt, and indeed of any suicidal act. Such a definition was proposed earlier in this chapter (p. 82). It really implies that any

* This is the description in physiological terms of death through hanging.

act of self-damage inflicted deliberately which looks like a suicidal attempt ought to be regarded and treated as such. Only if there is evidence that the person took no risk subjectively should the act be regarded as falling outside the categories of suicidal acts. This kind of definition leaves plenty of scope for the study of the great variety of behaviour patterns subsumed under the terms of suicidal act, suicidal attempt and suicide. The present author advises workers in this field to accept a basic proposition which he has found helpful. *Most people who commit suicidal acts do not either want to die or to live; they want to do both at the same time, usually the one more, or much more, than the other.* It is quite unpsychological to expect people in states of stress, and especially vulnerable and emotionally unstable individuals who form the large majority of those prone to acts of self-damage, to know exactly what they want and to live up to St James' exhortation: 'Let your yea be yea and your nay, nay'.

8

Ten years ago, in a W.H.O. publication, statistical data about suicide were described as the most clear-cut numerical facts in the whole field of psychiatry. This statement has to be taken with a grain of salt, for reasons outlined earlier in this book (p. 24). The frequency of open verdicts in coroners' courts shows that it is sometimes difficult to establish suicide as the cause of death. But whatever the shortcomings of suicide statistics, they at least remain fairly constant in a community. Numerical data about suicidal attempts can claim no similar respectability. While in England and Wales every case of suicide has to be certified and registered and is subject to a coroner's inquest, there is no machinery for the registration of suicidal attempts. It is true that until 1961 attempted suicide was an offence against the law and all cases ought to have been reported to the police, but only a small proportion of cases came to their knowledge and not all of them were prosecuted (see p. 71). The number of cases of attempted suicide registered as such by the police used to be smaller than the number of suicides, an obvious absurdity. How, then, can one arrive at an estimate of their real incidence?

A large proportion of suicidal attempts are sent to hospitals. They are usually first seen in the casualty department whence many of them are admitted to one of the wards. The suicidal attempt is not always mentioned in the diagnostic return, especially if the patient suffers from a physical or mental illness. In order to establish, under present conditions, the number of patients admitted to hospital during one year because of a suicidal attempt, it is necessary to read through all case notes, which is a formidable task.

Another source of information is the general practitioner whose cooperation has to be sought. The simplest method of inquiry is a questionnaire. A survey covering hospitals and general practitioners should ascertain most cases of attempted suicide seen by doctors in a certain area. An inquiry of this kind carried out at Sheffield in 1960/61 revealed that about twenty per cent of the suicidal attempts seen by general practitioners had not been sent to hospital. There is an additional number of suicidal attempts which are not seen by any doctor at the time. Not infrequently, patients admitted to hospital after a suicidal attempt report previous attempts when no doctor had been called in. The size of this group is impossible to estimate, but it is probably not negligible.

Investigation into the incidence of attempted suicide is a time-consuming and tedious undertaking which requires the cooperation of a number of people. It is not surprising, therefore, that only two such inquiries have so far been completed, one at Los Angeles and the other at Sheffield. Another such survey is taking place at Edinburgh.

These surveys suggest that in the United Kingdom and in the United States the number of suicidal attempts is six to ten times that of the suicides, at least in urban communities.* This means that an English city of half a million inhabitants with a suicide rate of thirteen per 100,000, which is above the national average of eleven, would have 390–750 suicidal attempts per year. The number of suicidal attempts in Metropolitan London, with a population of over eight million, would be in the region of 7,500 to 12,500. Considering the large number of attempted suicides admitted to hospital, these figures do not seem to be overestimates. Admission rates of suicidal attempts vary through the year. They appear to be highest in the spring, which is also the peak period for suicides and depressive illness. The total number of people who attempt suicide in England and Wales within a year has been

*At Basle, Switzerland, the number of suicidal attempts per annum was in 1962 found to be ten to fifteen times that of suicides.

Table 11. Age and Sex Distribution of 639 Attempted Suicides. The Numbers in Parentheses Refer to Suicides. (*Brit.Med.J.*, 2, p.137, 1965.)

Year	Sex	<20	20–29	30–39	40–49	50–59	60–69	70–79	80+	Total
1960 {	M	10	29 (1)	27 (4)	17 (4)	14 (6)	11 (7)	9 (2)	5(3)	122
	F	25	28	43 (2)	34 (3)	28 (5)	19 (1)	12	9(1)	198
1961 {	M	11	24	24 (4)	20 (1)	13 (6)	4 (5)	10(4)	5(1)	111
	F	28	41	32 (1)	32(11)	29 (6)	23 (5)	16(3)	7	208
		74	122(1)	126(11)	103(19)	84(23)	57(18)	47(9)	26(5)	639

assumed to be between 30,000 and 40,000. Some of them are likely to have made more than one attempt in that period.

The sex and age composition of this population differs from that of the suicides. More men than women kill themselves, but more women than men attempt suicide. *The peak age for suicides* has usually been found to lie between fifty-five and sixty-four, and for *attempted suicides* between twenty-four and forty-four. These data are important for the rough estimate of the number of people alive who at some time have attempted suicide, that is presented at the end of Chapter 10.

Table 11 shows the sex and age distribution among all suicidal attempts admitted to hospitals and among the suicides registered in Sheffield during a period of two years. The number of non-fatal suicidal acts which occurred in the city in that time was, of course, greater by at least one fifth (see above). The age group 'under 20' consisted only of persons admitted to wards for adults. Children's wards were not included in this inquiry. The table shows that the ratio between non-fatal and fatal suicidal acts declined with age, but tended to increase after the age of 70. There was no age group in which the non-fatal suicidal acts were not at least three times as frequent as the fatal ones. It was purely accidental that in the two years surveyed there was only one suicide under the age of 30 in the city. In other two year periods there had been a few.

Since the above survey was carried out by Parkin and Stengel, there has been a marked increase of suicidal attempts, but not of suicides, in many countries. The ratio of non-fatal to fatal suicidal acts can be assumed to be much higher than it was found to have been in Sheffield in the early sixties. In Sheffield it doubled between 1960 and 1970 (A. J. Smith).

9

Methods used in Suicidal Attempts

The methods of self-destruction employed in fatal suicidal acts have been listed in Table 7 in Part I. The relative frequency of methods used in non-fatal suicidal acts is different, in that poisons other than domestic gas head the list. In Table 12 two groups of attempted suicides are compared with a group of suicides. The samples have been taken, slightly modified and calculated per 1,000, from the monograph by Stengel and Cook (1958). The list of methods is fuller than the one for suicide (p. 38), since poisoning has been broken down into four categories instead of two. The most important difference between the lists is the higher ranking of the more dangerous and violent methods in the fatal group. This is what one would have expected.

The two groups of suicidal attempts A1 and A2 differed in several respects. The percentage of narcotic poisonings was higher in the 1953 than in the 1946 sample. This might have been due to the fact that the National Health Service, introduced in 1948, made it easier to obtain narcotics. The increase in poisonings with narcotics was associated with a decline in the number of cases of suicidal gas poisoning, which is by far the most dangerous method, and of jumping from heights and of hanging. Thus, the easier availability of narcotics may help to reduce the number of fatal suicidal acts or to prevent it from rising steeply. In this country aspirin poisoning for example is relatively more frequent than elsewhere: it is extremely rare in the Scandinavian countries. The reason for this difference is probably that aspirin is offered for sale almost everywhere in the United Kingdom.

Table 12. Methods (per 1,000) used by two groups of attempted suicides, A1, 1946 and A2, 1953, and in one group of suicides, B, 1953.

Group	A1, 1946		A2, 1953		B, 1953	
	Male	Female	Male	Female	Male	Female
Domestic gas	160	219	134	161	466	477
Other Poisons:						
Disinfectant	66	110	15	38	27	—
Narcotic	122	219	327	311	109	204
Aspirin	66	111	89	75	14	23
Others	11	—	45	85	27	—
Wounding	300	73	238	94	27	23
Train and Vehicle	23	24	29	47	55	23
Height	66	122	29	66	82	182
Hanging	133	73	29	47	82	45
Drowning	44	12	59	66	55	—
Shooting	—	—	—	—	41	—
Miscellaneous	9	37	6	10	15	23

The increase in deliberate self-poisonings, especially with narcotic drugs, has been referred to under the methods of suicide (p. 40). The increase is even more striking among the non-fatal suicidal acts. An official survey of hospital treatment of acute poisoning published in 1968 revealed that between 1957 and 1964 the hospital admissions for poisoning in England and Wales had increased threefold. About one in five people taking poison repeated the act within one year, usually within three months. This alarming increase in mostly suicidal self-poisonings has continued to be associated with a decline in suicides by coal gas and by other methods with a high lethality. The possible cause of this remarkable statistical relationship has been discussed in connexion with suicide.

What is the fate of people who have made suicidal attempts? Clinical impressions are rather confusing. To judge from the large number of not very dangerous attempts seen in hospitals and from the apparent triviality of precipitating causes, most people, one supposes, recover quickly from the incident, soon forget all about it, and have a normal expectation of life. However, many suicidal attempts are very serious and survival is often due only to accident. The impression here is that the suicidal act will be repeated before long, probably with fatal outcome, unless the patient is prevented from doing so. Of late, clinical impressions and hunches have become suspect because they have so often been proved wrong. This is why the need for careful follow-up investigation has been felt recently and why in several parts of the world such studies have been undertaken, independently of each other. If they are concerned with sizeable groups of people, they have been called 'cohort studies', after the unit of the Roman Legion; the investigator follows the progress of a band of people through life, noting which of them fall by the wayside, and watching the progress of the rest.

The technical difficulties of such studies are considerable, especially if the investigators want to interview every patient and, whenever possible, a relative. The tracing of the patients alone is a formidable task. In Great Britain there is no residential register and often much patience and ingenuity is needed to find a person with whom contact was lost several years previously. It requires a small team to carry out these investigations, of which the following are examples.

Group A1. All admissions for attempted suicide to a London psychiatric observation ward during the year 1946 were followed up five and six years later. Their number was 138, which was about ten per cent of the total number of admissions to the observation ward. Ninety had come from general hospital wards where they had been taken immediately after the suicidal attempt. Obviously all of them had been thought to be in need of specialized psychiatric observation. This series, therefore, did not include the type of suicidal attempt mentioned above that tends to give the impression of harmlessness and triviality. The composition of the group according to diagnosis of the mental condition underlying the suicidal attempts was as follows:

Schizophrenia	13
Depressive illness	49
Other abnormal depressions	45
Psychopathic personalities	21
Others	10

The proportion of patients suffering from a mental disorder requiring specialized psychiatric treatment was above average in this series compared with unselected groups. Even so, in the majority of this series the suicidal attempt had been precipitated by stressful experiences not arising from mental illness. In those cases the attempt had been carried out in a state of *reactive* (see p. 61) depression, which in a considerable number was due to physical illness. Thirty-five of the whole group were over sixty.

The group was atypical also in its sex composition, in that it consisted of seventy-four men and sixty-four women, but this might have been due to shortage of accommodation for females in that particular observation ward. Thirty-one patients (22.6 per cent) were living in social isolation, i.e. they had no fixed abode, or lived alone in lodgings. Only seven per cent of the general population live in that way. The proportion of single and widowed among this group was excessive. All religious denominations were represented. In nine of the women the mental disorder underlying the suicidal attempt was related to recent childbirth.

The biggest number of attempts, twenty, fell into the month of May, a typical finding for both suicides and attempted suicides. The methods used by this group of patients were listed in Table 12 under A1, calculated per 1,000 to make them comparable with the list of methods of suicide reproduced in Table 7. Thirty-one of the patients had made suicidal attempts previously. All but ten of the patients could be traced in 1951 and 1952. The mortality from natural causes after five years was twenty-six per cent, which was mainly due to the large proportion of aged sick whose expectation of life would have been low in any case. Only one patient of the whole group of 138 died through suicide, although a considerate minority had made a further attempt.

He was a widower, aged sixty-nine on admission to the observation ward in 1946 following a suicidal attempt. He came from a working-class family and was the eighth of nine siblings. His father died when the patient was a few years old, and this meant hardship for the family. He became an electrician. He married at the age of twenty. The marriage was not happy and he was jealous of his wife. He did not want any children of his own. He was solitary and had very few friends. After retirement he lived on his old-age pension and by letting rooms in his house. In 1945 his wife died and he lived on his own, refusing his sister's offer to live with him. She visited him regularly. Three days after an apparently trivial quarrel with her he attempted suicide by gassing. He was found unconscious by a tenant and was taken to the observation ward. There he stated that he had been depressed since his wife's death and more so just before the attempt. He wanted to take his life because he felt that nobody wanted him.

After a week he said that he felt no longer depressed and refused to go to a mental hospital voluntarily. It would have been impossible to transfer him against his will. He was discharged to friends who had offered him a home, but within three weeks he returned to his own house where his sister continued to visit him from time to time. Ten months later he gassed himself while his tenants were away. No precipitating cause could be found. Had the patient stayed in hospital longer, and had he accepted the suggestion that he should live with his sister or his family, the outcome might have been different. His suicidal attempt had failed to bring about a change in his life situation.

At the time of the inquiry only eighteen of the 138 patients were in a mental hospital, ten of whom had been there since 1946. Seventy-four patients were out of hospital. Twenty-four among those traced had made another suicidal attempt since 1946.

Group A2, consisted of seventy-six unselected patients admitted to a medium-sized general hospital in London after a suicidal attempt. Twenty-six were male and fifty female. Again, almost one quarter were over sixty. The diagnostic categories were as follows:

Schizophrenia	1
Depressive illness	20
Other abnormal depressions	45
Psychopathic personalities	8
Confusional states	2

This group is typical of the suicidal attempts admitted to general hospitals. Compared with group A1 it had a lower proportion of serious mental disorders.

No systematic follow-up of this group was carried out, but it became known that three of them, aged fifty-four, fifty-six, sixty-eight respectively, had killed themselves within two and a half years. Two of them had a serious physical illness and the third suffered from depressive illness.

These data show how much groups of patients who had made suicidal attempts differ, and that it is not possible to generalize from one or a few such groups. Probably none of them can be regarded as truly representative of the attempted suicides in the general population. To find a truly representative sample one would have to include those who are not admitted to hospital.

The upper social classes are under-represented among the attempted suicide groups and over-represented among the suicides. However, this difference is probably more apparent than real. If a suicidal attempt happens in a middle- or upper-class family, everything is done to hush it up and usually there is strong opposition to hospital admission. These attitudes are less marked in working-class families. As a result, members of the upper and middle classes are not as common among hospital admissions for attempted suicides as one would expect from the class distribution among suicides.

Follow-up studies carried out elsewhere and covering longer periods than the London investigations also show that only a small minority of people who make suicide attempts kill themselves later. The critical period seems to be the four years following the attempt. Dahlgren of Malmö, Sweden, found that of 237 suicidal attempts admitted to a general hospital from 1933 to 1942 about ten per cent had killed themselves by 1945, but his sample, too, was atypical and highly selective. It had more men than women and had a large proportion of alcoholics, whose suicide proneness is excessive. Schneider of Lausanne found a similar incidence of suicides among people who had attempted suicide up to eighteen years previous to the date of his study. All these findings indicate that the large majority of people who make suicidal attempts are likely to survive. However, the incidence of suicides among them is far higher than in comparable groups of the general population who have no history of suicidal attempts. This must never be forgotten when the results of cohort studies of attempted suicides are considered. *People who have attempted suicide present a highly vulnerable group with an excessive suicidal risk.* The criteria of this risk in individuals will be discussed later.

Now we are in a position to ask how many people have at least once in their lives made a suicidal attempt. If we accept the estimates of 60,000 to 80,000 suicidal attempts per year in the United Kingdom, and remember that the majority of them are between twenty-five and forty-five years of age, and that only a small minority of them are going to kill themselves while the rest have probably the same expectation of life as comparable age groups of the general population, it can be assumed that at any given time their number cannot be less than half a million, though it may be bigger. (Dublin's estimate for the United States is two millions.) This is a sizeable section of the total population. It would mean that in this country every general practitioner must have about ten to twenty such people among his clientele. It would be important to identify them because they are in need of special attention. However, unless the doctor has himself intervened in a suicidal attempt, he is unlikely to know which of his patients belong to this group, because attempts tend to be concealed by the patients and their relatives as something to be ashamed of.

Various methods of assessing with some degree of precision the risk of suicide in individuals who had made a suicidal attempt have been proposed. Tuckman and Youngman, working in Philadelphia, adopted death from suicide within a year following the attempt as the criterion of risk, which greatly limits the value of the method. They isolated 14 risk-related factors, most of them identical with those listed earlier in this book (p. 61). Poeldinger subjected a large sample of patients admitted to the Psychiatric University Clinic at Basle following a suicidal attempt to a statistical analysis in which 35 risk-related factors and their mutual correlations measurable on a three-point scale were tabulated. For instance, in one of his patients who later killed herself, 14 of the 35 factors had been present. The degree of their mutual correlations in a suicide-prone population was also noted. One of the factors was social isolation. Its correlations to the other factors were added together, and the same was done with the other 12 factors. The sum total of those correlation figures was 137, called the risk figure. It was found that any figure above 100 indicated a high risk and called for hospitalization. The author claims that his method of assessing suicidal risk conveys more than other assessments which take into account only the number of risk-related factors present, and not also their mutual interrelationship which often adds considerably to the weight of the single factor. It goes without saying that in clinical practice the doctor will not rely on these methods of assessment alone, but they are valuable nevertheless. They serve as reminders of the large varieties of factors involved and embody the collective experience of others, though as it were in 'potted' form.

For and Against Self
                                    Destruction

Most suicidal acts show certain features which are not compatible
with or even opposed to the purpose of self-destruction. They are
obvious in many suicidal attempts, but they can be discerned in
suicides also. Careful retrospective inquiry reveals that the large
majority of people who commit suicidal acts, fatal and non-fatal,
have given a *warning* of their intention to do so. This warning
may range from only an expression of a wish to be dead, or a hint
of self-destructive intention, to an outspoken threat or a deliberate
statement. Whatever the form of these communications, they
served, or could have served, as an indication of suicidal intention. In all such cases in which preventive action was possible the
suicidal act would not have taken place if the warnings had been
taken seriously.

   Most suicidal attempts are carried out in a setting which makes
intervention of others possible, probable, or even inevitable.
People who attempt suicide tend to remain near to others, and
thus allow for the possibility of rescue. At least, it can be said
that only in a very few suicidal attempts were precautions against
that possibility taken. But whether or not other people will
intervene is usually left to chance.

   The social constellation of suicidal attempts varies a lot but in
most cases tends to favour survival. In Tables 13 and 14 two
series of suicidal acts have been analysed to show how near other
people were at the time of the act. Group A2 consisted of sixty-
six men and 101 women who attempted suicide, group B of

seventy-three men and forty-four women who committed suicide. There was no marked difference in the methods used by those who were alone as compared with the group as a whole. It is clear that the social constellation at the time of the act favoured survival in group A more than in group B, but even among the latter there was a considerable proportion of cases who with some luck might have survived, i.e. those whose suicides were committed in much frequented public places, at home with other people present or even in the same room (Table 14). The two groups differ in the proportions listed under 'alone in house', but even there intervention was not impossible and quite a few of group B might have survived had an unexpected visitor turned up or an expected person not have been delayed.

Table 13 shows the degree of isolation during the suicidal acts of groups A2 and B. It refers to the kind of person, if any, near to the patient at the time of the attempt. 'Special persons' were people related to the patient by family bonds, by close acquaintance, or by occupation. A person was described as 'near' when he was under the same roof with the patient or otherwise in close reach. 'In company' means being together with the patient. 'No relevant data' refers to cases in which the precise geographical relationship between those persons and the individual who committed the suicidal act could not be ascertained retrospectively, but those persons were known to have been in some way involved in the act. They may have been expected to be near, but had in fact been absent at the time, and so forth.

The analysis of the *agents who intervened* in the suicidal act, and thus secured or helped in the patient's survival, shows that frequently it is the suicidal individual himself who intervenes. No similar data are available for suicides, but it is known to happen also in fatal cases though without success. Table 15 refers to group A2. The various categories are self-explanatory. 'No information' refers to the lack of information as to how the person who intervened had appeared on the scene.

The observations recorded in this section concern manifest behaviour rather than thought contents and emotional state. These will be dealt with in the section dealing with the psycho-

Table 13. Degree of isolation during suicidal act (figures in brackets are the numbers of patients).

	Group A2 (attempts)		Group B (suicides)	
	Men (66)	Women (101)	Men (73)	Women (44)
Special person near	11	16	16	5
Special person in company	5	4	—	—
Special person no relevant data	2	2	—	—
Others near	20	32	26	8
Others in company	6	4	—	—
Others no relevant data	—	4	—	—
Alone	14	30	30	31
Unknown	8	9	1	—

Table 14. Sites of suicidal acts in relation to other people.

	Group A2 (attempts)		Group B (suicides)	
	Men (66)	Women (101)	Men (73)	Women (44)
Much frequented public place	15	16	5	1
Little frequented public place	3	4	5	2
Others present in house or flat	18	36	16	7
Others in same room	9	7	2	2
Alone in house, flat or work place	14	30	44	32
Unknown	7	8	1	—

dynamics of attempted suicide. Perhaps the behavioural peculiarities described above have been neglected until recently because the students of suicidal acts were guided solely by what the patients said about themselves and their actions. Here, as in other fields of human psychology, the study of overt behaviour can draw attention to certain aspects of which the individual under observation is not, or only incompletely, aware. The various features of the suicidal act as a behaviour pattern indicate

Table 15. Agents intervening.

| | Group A2 (attempts) | |
	Men (66)	Women (101)
Patient	19	24
Special person (expected)	6	9
Special person (accidentally)	9	6
Special person (no information)	—	5
Others (expected)	—	3
Others (accidentally)	18	35
Others (no information)	6	4
Unknown	8	15

that it is not only directed towards destruction and death but also towards human contact and life. This is why it has been described as Janus-faced.

There are people, some of them hysterics, schizophrenics, or epileptics, who have a history of repeated suicidal attempts. They may try to kill themselves as often as three or four times a year. This behaviour either ends in suicide or ceases after some time, especially if there has been a change in the patient's life situation, such as a move into a protective environment.

The fact that many acts of self-damage are harmless to life, that suicidal intent is often denied, and that the purpose of manipulation of the environment is often admitted, makes it doubtful whether it is justified to describe such acts as 'attempted suicide'. This designation seems to imply that there always is conscious intention of self-destruction in the absence of opposing tendencies, and it does not do justice to the complexity of the underlying motivations described in chapter 13. On the other hand, 'attempted suicide' has the advantage of directing attention to the self-destructive component, which may be latent, and to the suicide proneness of those people which is evidenced by their excessive suicide rate. The term 'pseudocide' (Lennard-Jones and Asher) has been proposed for apparently harmless acts of self-damage, but this term denies the presence of the suicidal component, quite apart from the semantic ambiguity of the word which could also mean pseudohomicide. Recently Kessel proposed 'self-poisoning' for these acts, but this is again an ambiguous description because it says nothing about the outcome. That author is of the opinion that in the majority of cases the act of self-poisoning has nothing to do with suicide, although sometimes it may be fatal by accident. He regards this kind of behaviour to be only demonstrative and manipulative, and he refuses to assume a concealed or an unconscious or preconscious tendency to self-destruction playing a part in them, even though the self-poisoner may take considerable risks. He is much impressed by the impulsive nature of the majority of these acts of self-damage, which to him indicates that they are not suicidal attempts. It can be argued against this approach that on closer questioning one almost invariably finds a recent history of suicidal thoughts in those cases, that the patients' statements about their intentions are often no reliable guide to the meaning of their actions, that apparently harmless and purely manipulative acts of self-poisoning are not infrequently followed by more dangerous acts whose self-destructive purpose is admitted, and that there has been a marked increase of the suicide rates in the younger age groups in which the increase of non-fatal self-poisoning is highest. Greer and Lee found that the incidence of suicide within one to four and a half years following potentially lethal attempts did not differ significantly from the incidence observed in unselected samples which had been followed up and among which there had been many not medically dangerous acts. These findings should serve as a warning against taking apparently harmless acts of self-damage lightly.

12   The Psychological and Social Effects of Attempted Suicide

What are the effects of attempted suicide on the individual concerned and on the human environment? It is strange that this question has only recently been asked for the first time. The effects are complex and varied. The following are some typical changes brought about by the suicidal attempt in the person's life situation.

Temporary hospitalization and treatment is the most common consequence of a non-fatal suicidal act in our society. (Patients who die in hospital as the result of the suicidal act which led to their admission are not included here. They are classed as suicides.)

The duration of stay in hospital varies considerably. Of the 138 patients admitted to a psychiatric observation ward in 1946, seventy-six were discharged in less than three months and only ten were still in a mental hospital five years after the attempt. The discharge rate is even higher and the stay in hospital shorter in patients admitted to a general hospital after a suicidal attempt and not transferred to a psychiatric hospital.

Some of the patients admitted after a suicidal attempt were under psychiatric out-patient treatment at the time, possibly because they refused in-patient treatment recommended by their doctors. In those cases the suicidal attempt results in hospital treatment which the patients had previously been unwilling to accept. But this is usually a small group compared with those who were not under psychiatric treatment at the time of the attempt although they had been mentally ill for some time. The suicidal attempt brings them to the attention of the psychiatrist and thus secures them the required specialist treatment: fifty-five out of the 138 patients belonging to group A1 (p. 95) were of this type. They had for some time before the suicidal attempt suffered from psychiatric symptoms which either had not been diagnosed as such or had been ignored. This is common in depressive illness the symptoms of which are often overlooked or misinterpreted. The following two cases* are typical of many.

Mrs A.B., born 1900, a war widow with a big family, had been in good health until early in 1946 when she complained about abdominal pain. She was thoroughly investigated physically, with negative results. She became very depressed and lost a great deal of weight. Following a trivial quarrel with a neighbour she drank a relatively harmless cleansing fluid with suicidal intent. By then her depression had been present for at least four months. Now her doctor recognized the seriousness of her condition and strongly advised her to enter a hospital for psychiatric treatment. As she adamantly refused to do so she was taken to the psychiatric observation ward without her consent. She was found to be deeply depressed and agitated and was convinced that she was suffering from incurable cancer. Again she refused to have treatment and she had to be transferred to a mental hospital as a certified patient. Under appropriate treatment she made a complete recovery within four weeks and was discharged perfectly well. Up to the time of the follow-up inquiry five years later she had remained in good health physically and mentally.

In this case the suicidal attempt had acted as an alarm signal. There was no correspondence between the seriousness of the mental illness and the degree of danger involved in the method of self-injury.

Mr F.C., aged forty-six, a clerk, became depressed and excessively preoccupied with his physical health. He tried to gas himself and was taken to hospital unconscious. He was found to

*The brief case-records presented in this book are masked in such a way that they cannot be identified by those who knew the patients and probably not even by the patients themselves.

be suffering from a depressive illness and given appropriate treatment. Four months after the suicidal attempt he was discharged recovered. His relationship with his wife improved greatly. He had always been a somewhat inadequate man with ambitions out of his reach. Whereas previously there had been a great deal of quarrelling with his wife, who was dissatisfied with his failure to achieve promotion, she now accepted him as he was. They became more tolerant of each other and spent much more time together than previously. They used to spend their holidays separately, now they went on holiday together. The patient's wife felt that his suicidal attempt rather than his depressive illness had made a powerful impact on her and was responsible for her change of attitude towards him. He accepted his modest professional status and became an active member of a Church to which his father had belonged.

In this case the suicidal attempt resulted in hospital treatment followed by recovery. It also contributed to an improvement in the patient's relationship with his wife.

The following case is representative of those patients whose suicidal attempts lead to effective treatment of physical illness. Mr F.L. had a stroke in 1942 at the age of sixty. His condition improved but he was unable to work. His wife had to go out to work, which worried him greatly. In May 1946 his depression got worse and he was convinced that he had only a few days to live. In a state of acute depression with confusion, he tried to gas himself and to cut his throat. His wife found him in time and he was taken to hospital, where heart failure was diagnosed. His heart condition was treated successfully and within two weeks he was cheerful and sleeping well. He was transferred from the psychiatric observation ward to a medical ward and finally discharged after three months. After his suicidal attempt his wife's employers who had learned about it gave her a pension and she no longer needed to go out to work. Now she could be with him all the time. He had no further depressions and was out of bed most of the time until his sudden death six months after his discharge from hospital.

In this case the suicidal attempt resulted in adequate treatment of physical illness and consequent recovery from associated psychiatric symptoms. In addition, his wife was given the opportunity to change her mode of life to be able to give him the maximum aid and comfort.

Permanent hospitalization follows a suicidal attempt in certain cases of mental or physical illness. The following is a case of mental illness where the suicidal attempt marked a turning point in the patient's life by demonstrating to him and to others his inability to live at home.

A sixty-year-old man had been suffering from a depressive illness for two years without seeking medical help. Having given up hope of recovery he tried to drown himself but was rescued. He was admitted to a mental hospital where he was found to be suffering from chronic depression and premature intellectual impairment. He settled down in the protective environment of the hospital and when interviewed six years after admission he was only mildly depressed although intellectual impairment was obvious. He would have been unable to live outside hospital.

Death from longstanding physical illness within a few weeks or months following the suicidal attempt is not uncommon. In some patients the attempt appears to be a last spontaneous act before passive surrender to natural death. Had they died in the act it could have been said of them that through committing suicide they had evaded natural death. Having survived, they have to accept it, and they usually do so without mental struggle. Most of these patients, when committing a suicidal act, are aware that they have only a short time to live. In consequence of the suicidal attempt, they spend the last period of their lives in hospital.

So far, reference has been made only to changes brought about by suicidal attempts of sick people. The majority of suicidal attempts, however, are committed by people in distress who are not ill in the accepted sense. What changes, if any, take place in their life situations subsequent to their suicidal attempts?

Removal from the scene of conflict is a very common immediate result. A short stay in hospital, even without special treatments, usually makes a great deal of difference to the person concerned. It means a sojourn in a sympathetic environment and tends to mobilize the resources of the personality.

The community comes to the aid of many persons who make a suicidal attempt, by providing not only medical but also material help and counselling. There have been cases in the United Kingdom in which a suicidal attempt has even hastened the allocation of a council house or flat.

Changes in human relationships and in modes of life frequently follow the crises which culminated in the suicidal attempts. A great variety of such changes can be observed and they often affect not only the person who committed the attempt but also those close to him. The relationship to the spouse, parent or other close relatives sometimes improves. The attempt may prevent a threatening break. In other cases, it may hasten the end of a relationship, especially when the bond is tenuous. While many a suicidal attempt has kept a family together, the boy-friend is likely sooner or later to take to flight when faced with this dire threat.

Another change which sometimes follows a suicidal attempt is the acceptance of dependence on others, which usually means a return to a previous dependent relationship. A typical example is the young person who returns to the parental home following a suicidal attempt. Other changes in a person's mode of life may concern his work and his social and economic commitments. The suicidal attempt may have repercussions on other people's modes of life. Typical examples are the husband on shiftwork who changes his job so that his wife is not left alone overnight, or the wife who stops going out to work in order to look after her sick husband.

The following two cases illustrate the profound effect a suicidal attempt can have on human relations:

Mrs A.B., aged thirty-two, was admitted to a general hospital after attempting to gas herself. She would not have been found alive if the occupant of the adjoining flat had not returned from her holiday a few days earlier than planned. She smelled gas on the landing, forced the door into the patient's flat and found her in the kitchen unconscious. She was in the flat alone. Her husband who was away on business was expected back only two days later. The patient left a lengthy letter explaining her motive. There could be no doubt about the seriousness of her suicidal intention.

It emerged that this woman, who was highly intelligent and held an important secretarial post, had for many years suffered from neurotic anxiety about which she had never consulted a doctor. She had been brought up fairly strictly. At the age of sixteen she had a short love affair, without sexual intercourse, but with a good deal of sex play. From that time onwards she had the fear of having contracted venereal disease. She believed that people suffering from such a disease could not have healthy children. She did not dare to reveal her fears to anybody in case they should be confirmed. Whenever she felt ill or noticed a blemish in her complexion, her fears became manifest. She married at the age of twenty-four and persuaded her husband that they ought to have no children, to enable her to continue with her secretarial work. Their marriage was happy at first, but her refusal to have a family cast a shadow over their relationship. A week before the suicidal attempt they had another inconclusive talk about this problem. She felt that she could no longer keep her secret from him, but was unable to tell him why she did not want to have children. When he was away she decided to take her life.

The patient responded well to psychotherapy. She continued to be over-anxious at times but completely lost the fear of venereal disease. She resumed her work four weeks after the suicidal attempt. She had her first child a year later and another child after an interval of two years. She proved a capable mother and when seen five years after the suicidal attempt she and her husband said that their family life was entirely happy. They believed that they owed their happiness to the psychiatric treatment the patient received following the suicidal attempt.

In this case the suicidal attempt had far-reaching effects. It brought to a head and revealed a long-standing crisis the existence of which the patient had concealed from everybody. It resulted in the resolution of this crisis with the help of treatment and in a profound change of her and her husband's life. It set in motion a sequence of events which led to the foundation of a family. It did so by mobilizing the resources of society appropriate to the solution of this particular problem. It is rare for the appeal effect of a suicidal act to be as complete and enduring as it was in this case.

Mrs R. S., a twenty-seven-year-old woman, was admitted to hospital following a serious suicidal attempt with hypnotics. She had married at the age of twenty-two, but divorced her husband, who was an alcoholic, after three years. She took a job as a postwoman. A year later she started a love affair with a bachelor ten years older than herself. He refused to marry her because he lived with his aged mother whom he did not want to leave. There were frequent quarrels between the two lovers and finally she decided to break off the relationship. Two weeks after they had parted she tried to kill herself. She had not communicated with him. He was deeply shocked when he learned by accident about her suicidal attempt. He immediately visited her in hospital and they came to a reconciliation. Their relationship was resumed and three months later they got married, his mother having decided to live with a sister. Five years after the suicidal attempt the marriage appeared to be happy.

A change in social isolation often follows a suicidal attempt. Not infrequently people who lived alone enter a family group or some other community following the attempt. The hospital or an old people's home are such communities. Considering the importance of social isolation among the factors contributing to suicidal acts, this is a significant change in a person's life.

All the effects of suicidal attempts listed above seem to mean that the person's life situation improves. The gain, however, is often transient and in some cases there is an early return to the previous unsatisfactory situation which may lead to a recurrence of the suicidal act. This may continue until a real change in the person's relationship with the human environment takes place. Whether or not this happens depends on the personality of the individual concerned as well as on other people. There are abnormal persons who tend to discourage and inhibit helpful reactions by their aggressive behaviour or their inability to respond to kindness. In some cases the suicidal attempt leads to a final rupture of what are already crumbling relationships. This outcome is usually accepted and the suicidal attempt is credited with 'having cleared the air'.

Punitive reactions to the suicidal attempt rarely occur between individuals. However, it sometimes happens that relatives are angry and regard the suicidal attempt as an act directed against them, especially if it is not the first.

Until 1961, when attempted suicide ceased to be an indictable offence under the English Law, society reacted with punitive measures to attempted suicide, or at least threatened to do so. As similar laws still exist in some parts of the world it is of interest to recall what form the punitive reactions used to take in this country. The capricious way in which the law was implemented has already (p. 71) been referred to.

The police got to know about only a fraction of the cases, mainly those for which they were asked to call an ambulance, and, of course, the attempts carried out outside homes. Whether or not a charge was made depended on local police practice and this varied considerably. Most of the accused were bound over on condition that they attended a clinic for treatment. Prison sentences were sometimes given to people who had made suicidal attempts before, especially if there was nobody to take charge of them. Thus the law tended to discriminate against the person without relatives and friends. There was no evidence that the law had a deterrent effect on those convicted or on others.

The most recent study into the long-term effects of attempted suicide is Retterstöl's personal follow-up of a sample of cases.

13   The Psychodynamics of
the Attempt

The motives and causes underlying suicidal attempts are in essence the same as those of suicide, although they may appear different if the intent to impress or hurt other people is more conspicuous than the urge to self-destruction. The fact of survival makes the suicidal attempt a different behaviour pattern from suicide and a meaningful and often a momentous event in a person's life. The meaning it acquires to the individual depends on a variety of circumstances. The role of other people in the causation of the fatal suicidal act is not always obvious. In the non-fatal act they often come into the picture as objects of love and hate, during and after the attempt. A psychodynamic examination of attempted suicide cannot ignore the interpersonal aspects of the act itself. Aggression directed against others is more manifest in suicidal attempts than in suicide. Yet often a wish to seek contact is also noticeable. The manifestations of these conflicting intentions have been described in the fictitious report of an unprejudiced observer (pp. 77-9).

Some warning of suicidal intention has almost invariably been given. Those who attempt suicide tend, in the suicidal act, to remain near or move towards other people. Suicidal attempts act as alarm signals and have the effect of an appeal for help, even though no such appeal may have been consciously intended.

The awareness of the *appeal effect* on the part of those who attempt suicide varies a great deal. Hysterical and psychopathic personalities tend to exploit it while most others do not appear to think of it at the time of the suicidal attempt. It is by virtue of its appeal effect that the suicidal attempt so often leads to a change in the person's life situation. This is probably one of the reasons why suicidal attempts are only rarely repeated immediately.

The appeal effect of a suicidal attempt on relatives and friends is derived from the guilt feelings it creates in them, even if they do not feel directly responsible for it. Society reacts in the same way. The guilt feelings experienced by others in this situation have been regarded as reactions to conscious or unconscious death-wishes towards the person who tried to take his life. There is often ample cause for such guilt feelings, because people who are sufficiently loved and cared for do not attempt to take their lives unless they are mentally ill.

The psychological effects of the suicidal attempt on those close to the person who tried to take his life have a relationship to *grief reactions*. What are the effects of bereavement on people close to the deceased? There is usually an upsurge of posthumous love, or at least of tender feelings towards him; a sense of guilt for not having loved him enough and not having done enough for him; regret that it is too late to make good. If death was due not to natural causes, but to suicide, these reactions are much more pronounced, especially if the bereaved feels that he could have prevented the death or that he was partly or wholly responsible for it. When, as frequently happens, he had conscious death wishes against the deceased person, the self-reproach is even stronger. But there are some significant differences in the case of suicidal attempt. Those close to the person who *almost* died, usually feel an upsurge of love or at least some tender feelings towards him. But while in the case of a fatal outcome it is too late to make amends, in the case of attempted suicide amends can be made by them and they feel an urge for compensation and reparation. This urge is the stronger the greater the guilt feelings are. In fact, people close to the person who attempted suicide, and society, try to behave as they would have felt they ought to have behaved had the outcome been fatal. This appears to be an important motive for the helpful reactions that follow suicidal attempts. These reactions may be short-lived and abortive, but they are almost invariably present. They seem to be common to all cultures. Some such response from the environment is a predictable effect of every suicidal attempt. This is why a suicidal attempt acts as an appeal, as a cry for help. Every suicidal attempt has an appeal function.

The notion of the appeal effect, or appeal function, has frequently been misunderstood. It has mistakenly been limited to consciously intended cries for help, and attempts at manipulation, which, as far as this can be ascertained, applied only to a small minority of suicidal acts. If one misunderstands the notion in this way it is only logical to deny its general significance. But if one considers the effect of a suicidal act on other people, the presence or absence of conscious intention of achieving such a response is not decisive. On the contrary, the appeal effect of a suicidal act may be the greater the less it was intended. Whatever its conscious motivation, the suicidal act is a powerful communication of distress. It owes its effect on others to their responses which have been described above. In this sense, it is perfectly legitimate to speak of an appeal effect, or appeal function, of physical illness in whose causation the sick person has no part. The difference between the appeal effects of physical illness and of suicidal acts lies in the character of the latter which are voluntary actions chosen by individuals.

The misunderstanding described here is due to the difficulty many people have in considering motives which are not clearly conscious, and also to the assumption that every action has only one motive. Therefore, a suicidal act must aim either at appealing for help or at death. That both motives can be present at the same time, though in different strengths, seems to many difficult to comprehend. Also, there is the preference of the simple to the complex, and the impatience of some psychiatrists with those who look behind the surface of human behaviour. 'In the face of the obvious and simple, they cleave to the complicated, fortified against the evidence by the concept of unconscious ambivalence' (Kessel), the evidence being the attempter's statement about his motives. This approach is at variance with the views held by the author of this book who has always warned against being taken in by the apparent simplicity of risk-taking self-damage.

The question is often asked what a suicidal act is an appeal for, if it cannot alter the conditions which led to it. Usually for nothing specific, just for help. It says no more and no less than 'I want to die – or *do* something for me', even though everything possible may have been done. The emphasis in this double message varies.

Uncertainty of outcome, i.e. from the point of view of the person committing the act, is a common feature of most suicidal acts. This is why they have been likened to a *gamble with life* which has come off (Weiss). Some suicidal attempts have been compared with Russian Roulette, a particularly dangerous kind of gamble in which survival depends entirely on chance. Few suicidal attempts are carefully planned. Their outcome depends not only on the balance between the life-preserving and self-destructive tendencies within the individual, two highly variable quantities, but on a variety of unknown factors, such as the potency of the poison taken and the possibility of intervention from the environment, its timing, efficacy, etc. Many suicidal attempts can even more aptly be compared with an *ordeal*, which is a specific type of gamble with life. The term 'ordeal' is here used in its ancient ritual meaning, i.e. of a trial in which a person submitted himself, or was subjected, to a dangerous test the outcome of which was accepted as the judgement of the Deity. A schizophrenic patient, when asked about the motive for his suicidal attempt, said that it was an act of faith: he wanted to prove whether God wanted him to live or to die. Others are less clear about this and simply say: 'I was fed up and took the tablets. I wanted to see what happens', or something to this effect. Survival is usually accepted without demur, for some time at least.

Uncertainty of outcome characterizes premeditated as well as impulsive suicidal acts. It is often believed that the latter need not be taken seriously because they are thought to be precipitated by the situation rather than by conscious suicidal intent. However, closer psychological examination of such attempts usually reveals previous suicidal thoughts.

The release of aggressive impulses directed against the self in an emotional outburst may have a beneficial *cathartic effect* on a person's mental state, i.e. it may relieve pent-up tension and thus restore emotional equilibrium, at least temporarily. This is possibly one of the reasons why some people feel much improved following a suicidal attempt and why they do not contemplate repeating it. It is difficult to prove this hypothesis because there often are other more obvious explanations for the improvement in the individual's life situation. Occasionally, however, the psychiatrist sees a dramatic recovery from a severe depressive illness as the result of a dangerous suicidal attempt. In those rare instances the method employed caused the patient to be deeply unconscious for several hours or days. It would be difficult to attribute the recovery in these cases to purely psychological processes. It is more likely to be due to an effect on the brain akin to that underlying the action of electric shock treatment on depressive illness. In that treatment, which is not dangerous, a remarkable improvement from severe depressive symptoms is brought about by inducing short periods of unconsciousness.

In the complex motivations of suicidal acts the urge for *self-punishment* is supposed to play a part. A suicidal attempt is sometimes experienced as a gratification of this urge and may thus contribute to a release of emotional tension. Many people feel guilty and are apologetic after a suicidal attempt. They are fairly clearly aware of its aggressive significance even if the wish to die was foremost in their minds.

Part III

Suicidal Acts Irrespective of Outcome

14   The Psychodynamics of
Suicidal Acts

In this book suicide and attempted suicide have so far been treated separately. This separation is artificial, but it was necessary because the conventional approach to suicidal acts has been unduly restricted to those that are fatal and has obscured important aspects of suicidal attempts. Now that these aspects have been demonstrated and discussed it is possible to view suicidal acts as a whole and irrespective of outcome. Their incidence is very high. In this country the total number of suicidal acts irrespective of outcome per 100,000 of the population might have been two to three hundred in 1970. These figures represent the suicide rate plus the attempted suicide rate. Suicidal acts differ by the amount of self-destructive intent and by the degree of risk taken. In this country only a small minority of suicidal acts have a fatal outcome. Apart from the small proportion of suicides in which safeguards against survival are taken, all suicidal acts are gambles with life with a more or less uncertain outcome. There is reason to believe that the impact they make on other people plays a part in the motivation of all suicidal acts, even if a fatal outcome is felt to be certain.

The risk-taking aspect of suicidal acts is illustrated by the suicide of the film star Marilyn Monroe. She had made several dangerous suicidal attempts before. She poisoned herself with narcotics in her home during the night. There were no signs of precautions against survival. On the contrary, her housekeeper was at home and might easily have come into her bedroom before it was too late. Marilyn Monroe was found dead clutching the telephone. Shortly before she took the poison she had had a talk with her doctor over the phone telling him of her depression and anxiety. She had been in the habit of doing this, with or without suicidal threats. On many previous occasions the doctor had come to her house during the night and managed to calm her down. That particular night he tried to do so by talking to her over the phone and made various suggestions for what she could do to get over her acute depression. He was criticized for not having gone to her house on that occasion as he had often done previously. It is easy to understand that if a patient becomes too demanding, appeals for help tend to lose their alarming effect.

The suicide of the London osteopath Stephen Ward in August 1963 which received world-wide publicity also illustrates the gamble character inherent in many suicidal acts. He was the centre of a society scandal and was standing trial on a charge of living on the immoral earnings of women. He had been allowed bail and appeared calm and confident throughout the court proceedings. On the night before the last day of the trial he took a large overdose of sleeping tablets. In the morning he was found unconscious by his host. He had left a note asking his friend to delay resuscitation and expressing the hope that he would not survive. He died in hospital several days later but only after his condition had taken an unexpected turn for the worse. The large majority of similar cases of intoxication survive today and Stephen Ward was obviously aware of this possibility. The posthumous effect of his suicide on public opinion is impossible to assess. Whatever sympathy he had among the general public probably increased, at least temporarily. It is doubtful whether the writers who in a famous letter to the press described him as a victim of hypocrisy would have done so had they not been moved by his suicide – if, that is, he had merely been convicted of the offences he had been charged with.

Another illustration of the risk factors on which the outcome of a suicidal act depends is proved by the following case. Mrs A.J., aged fifty, a widow, had been depressed for some weeks but had managed to attend to her business. One evening her son, who had come home from work as usual, heard an unusually loud snoring from her bedroom, went in and found her lying on her bed in her clothes, deeply asleep. He thought this peculiar but believed that his mother, who had been tired and sleepless lately, was having a good sleep at last. The young man was in a hurry to meet his fiancée, came home late and went to bed. In the morning his mother was found dead in the same position in which he had left her. Had he acted differently she would probably have survived and she would have been classified as a suicidal attempt.

Raymond Firth's observations on suicidal acts on a small Polynesian island, referred to earlier in this book (p. 66), are of considerable interest in this context. In his report published in 1961 under the title 'Suicide and Risk-taking in Tikopia Society' he said:

Involved in the suicide attempt is a distinct element of risk-taking. It is part of my argument that such risk-taking may be built into the structure of ideas about suicide, and may then have a bearing on the sociological interpretation of the volume of suicide.

The most common method of suicide, besides hanging, was for men to go out into the rough sea in a canoe and for women to swim out to face heavy seas and sharks. As soon as the news of a suicide swim or voyage became known, a fleet of canoes was organized and went out in search of the fugitive. The chances of these rescue operations depended on the weather, the time of day or night, the availability of a rescue fleet. At any rate, the potential suicide knew that the outcome of his escape into the sea was uncertain even if he may have hoped to be picked up. The returned 'suicide' voyager was welcomed back sympathetically. He was completely reintegrated with society, his effort at 'detachment' having failed; thus he succeeded in resolving his problem which was usually a conflict with a member of his family group. If the suicide was prevented, usually no further attempt was made. What such a person is really doing is gambling on natural hazards and on his credit with society. If either nature or society is against him – if the weather is bad or the searching fleet lethargic – he loses his life.

In 1929-52 only one out of four of those who went to sea with suicidal intent was rescued. There was no clear cut line between intending to kill oneself and not. There may be instead a scale of intention-cum-risk-taking.

The same can be said about the large majority of suicidal acts in our society. The incidence of suicide in Tikopia depended on the efficiency of the rescue procedures, i.e. on the suicide prevention service. A firmly structured and rigid society has good rescue procedures and a low suicide rate although the number of attempted suicides might be high. That kind of society does not readily permit one of its members to detach himself from it, by suicide or in any other way.

The urge to take risks, to incur hazards and to test fate appears to be a universal feature of human behaviour. Professor John Cohen of Manchester, who has made a penetrating study of the psychology of guessing and gambling, agrees

that it is possible to gain a better understanding of attempted suicide if we regard it as conveying a particular degree of uncertainty that the attempt will succeed or fail. The person's psychological probability of self-destruction may range from near certainty that he will die to near certainty that he will live.

However, Professor Cohen's subsequent statement that 'the true goal of attempted suicide is not self-destruction but survival' is misleading because those goals coexist though usually in different strengths. He probably means by 'true goal' the one that predominates and is likely to prevail. The crucial decision is left to God or Providence or Fate.

The origin of the urge to test fate or luck is obscure. Gambling in general has been regarded as a provocation of fate which is forced to make its decision for or against the individual. Fate has to decide, as psychoanalysts have put it, whether it loves the individual and wants to preserve him or hates him and wants to destroy him. Gambling and kindred risk-taking activities have been thought to originate from the urge to test the balance between love and life-preserving forces on the one hand and hate and destructive forces on the other hand. Some patients realize the gamble character of the suicidal act, for instance the schizo-phrenic mentioned above (p. 116). This patient's insight differed from that of most other people who attempt suicide only by his greater awareness of his motives.

The urge to test the balance between the forces derived from love and those derived from hate might be responsible for certain puzzling features of human behaviour. Children seem to be frequently engaged in the game of testing their parent's reactions to their misconduct, as if they wanted to find out exactly how much they are loved by testing how much their parents' love can stand. Possibly this common childhood behaviour pattern is the prototype of gambling.

Risk-taking behaviour pervades the life of adults too. It tends to endanger human relations and physical safety. The hazards incurred can vary greatly in the same individual. Professor Cohen has demonstrated by his experiments with bus drivers that alcohol induces people to incur greater hazards then when there is no alcohol in their bloodstream. These experiments are of particular interest for the student of suicidal acts, because the majority of these acts, fatal and non-fatal, carried out by men are committed after the consumption of alcohol, often only in small amounts. Thus the greater likelihood of both accidents and suicidal acts occurring under the influence of drink might be due to alcohol inducing people to incur greater hazards than usual. Here the intrinsic relationship between certain types of accidents and suicide is highly suggestive. Both originate from risk-taking behaviour and result in various degrees of hazards to life.

The picture of suicidal acts which emerges from these observa-tions is quite different from the popular idea of suicide and attempted suicide as rational and understandable behaviour pat-terns. An example of such a notion is that of the 'balance sheet suicide', popular on the Continent, i.e. of the mentally normal person who looks back on his life, draws the balance sheet of gains and losses, finds himself to be bankrupt and commits suicide. Something like this may go through the mind of a person suffering from depressive illness in which morbid guilt feelings and self-depreciation are prominent, but people who are not mentally ill do not behave so rationally. On the other end of the scale of suicidal acts there is the equally unrealistic picture of the suicidal attempt undertaken solely to exploit other people's soft-heartedness.

These and similar notions fail to do justice to the complexity of motivations underlying suicidal acts. There is always more than one reason for a suicidal act, whatever its manifest and conscious motive may be or may appear to have been. If people killed themselves only because they were tired of life, or if they endangered their lives only to get sympathy, the problem would not be why there are so many but why there are so few suicidal acts. Menninger thought that in committing suicide the individual killed himself, murdered somebody else and also fulfilled his wish to die. This formula certainly takes account of the aggressive components of the suicidal act, but there are, in addition, motivations which do not spring from the aggressive destructive drives but from those underlying human relations. There is the desire to bring about a change of other people's feelings towards one, if only posthumously, and also the urge to test fate, in the same way as some children want to find out whether their parents love or hate them. We therefore have to add to Menninger's triad the appeal and the ordeal function of the suicidal act. The two latter spring partly from the urge to self-preservation.

The suicidal act, then, is a highly complex behaviour pattern which reflects conflicting tendencies and whose outcome depends on their relative strength *and* on unpredictable factors. Because of the variety of motivations, of which a particular one may dominate the manifest situation in individual cases, suicidal acts can call forth all kinds of reactions from other people, from the deepest sympathy to anger and protest. An example of the latter type of reaction is given in the outcry of two American psychiatrists against the appeal effect and appeal function of the suicidal attempt.

Suicidal threats, other than psychotic reactions, pervade our entire social structure ... the threat of suicide forces people to marry, prevents marriage dissolution, coerces companionship between persons despite their mutual infidelity, prevents marriages, forces parents to acquiesce in their offspring's vicious habits, precludes admission to a mental institution, is rewarded by escape from military service, is used to obtain favoured treatment over siblings, is employed to avoid military induction, etc.

The authors obviously disapprove of the appeal effect of the suicidal act and imply that if it were disregarded few if any suicidal acts would be committed, at least none which do not serve solely the purpose of self-destruction. In excluding 'psychotic reactions', i.e. serious mental illness, they imply that in the suicidal acts of the mentally ill the appeal function plays no part. This view is mistaken.

Throughout the ages society has from time to time tried to counter the appeal of suicidal acts by posthumous humiliation of those who have committed suicide and by punishment of those who have attempted it. These measures have invariably failed and suicidal acts will continue to have an appeal function as long as they have an appeal effect, and that is a normal and indeed invariable consequence of the act. There is no point in protesting against this, even though it means that individuals and society are occasionally exposed to blackmail. Because of its effects on other people, the threat of suicide acts as one of the regulators of human relations in all societies in which suicide is dreaded and disapproved of. The only way to deprive it of its appeal effect is to make the appeal itself unnecessary.

One would at least expect suicidal attempts to be rare in a society indifferent or hostile to its individual members, if the appeal effect plays as important a part as has been assumed here. No such society now exists. Even in prison, a suicidal attempt calls forth reactions similar to those observed in the community at large. However, not long ago there existed a society which was openly hostile to its members, i.e. the German concentration camps. Several reports about the behaviour of the inmates have been published by medical observers who were themselves members of those communities. All of them noted the rarity of suicidal attempts. There was less agreement about the occurrence of suicide. Apart from 'occasional suicide epidemics' such as the one in which large numbers jumped to their deaths from a height, the common types of suicide were very rare. One of the observers, a distinguished psychiatrist, pointed out that to commit suicide one had only to approach the barbed wire to be shot dead, or one had only to relax in the struggle for survival to succumb rapidly. Some of these deaths might have been brought on with conscious suicidal intent. Another medical inmate explained the extreme rarity of manifest suicidal acts by the nature of the community which was experienced by many as a 'realm of death'. He believed that the main function of suicide was escape; whereas in a normal society one could escape from life by committing suicide, one could escape from death only by living. However this may be, the fact remains that attempted suicide, i.e. the type of suicidal act in which the appeal component is relatively strong, was extremely rare in those communities. This appears to support, at least negatively, the hypothesis of the appeal function of the suicidal attempt.

There are additional or alternative explanations for the rarity of manifest suicidal acts in the concentration camps. Possibly this phenomenon was due to the same factors as the decline of the suicide rates in war-time. This has never been explained satisfactorily. It might be due to several conditions: less social isolation, direction of aggressive feelings from the threatened self against the external enemy, and decline of the value of individual life.

In the prison population suicides and suicidal attempts do occur, but mainly in the early phases of imprisonment and in the period between arrest and sentence. Contrary to commonly held expectation, suicides are rare among long-term prisoners. The same applies to mentally ill criminals. Similar observations were made in prisoner-of-war camps where suicidal acts occurred chiefly in the early period of detention when adjustment to the environment had not yet been achieved.

In 1968 the occurrence of several suicides in an English prison reserved for persons on remand in custody awaiting trial received a good deal of public attention. This group is known to present the highest risk of suicide among the prison population.

In this book the concept of the suicidal act has been confined to behaviour motivated by self-destructive intention however vague and ambiguous. There is a wider concept which includes all kinds of behaviour involving self-damage with or without risk of death though not associated with conscious suicidal intent. Such behaviour patterns have been attributed partly or wholly to unconscious suicidal tendencies. Although this generalization may appear too sweeping there are types of risk-taking conduct, for instance persistent chain-smoking today, which suggest indifference to the preservation of life similar to the attitude underlying the less determined suicidal attempts. There are many accidents which cannot be understood without such an assumption.

Certain symptoms may serve as *suicidal equivalents*. It happens at times that a depressed person leaves home with a vague intention of taking his life. While he walks this intention fades and he keeps on walking in a dream-like state. He may find himself in a strange place after a few hours or days, having wandered many miles or travelled long distances. This state of 'fugue' or 'pathological wandering' is the best known example of the transformation of a suicidal drive into a different type of action in a state of altered consciousness. The emergence of this symptom can be regarded as a psychological defence mechanism against the suicidal impulse. It is not uncommon among a certain neurotic personality type.

*

The interplay of life-preserving with life-destroying tendencies, or of love and hate, pervades not only relations to other people but also to the self. They are reflected in the ideologies of death and in the complex motivations of suicidal acts. They truly mirror mankind's attitude to death, which has always meant the end as well as a new beginning.

Death has been seen as final extinction, as the gateway to eternal bliss, as punishment, as deliverance from and triumph over frailty and suffering, as the reunion with the beloved and as eternal peace. Suicide, accordingly, has meant all this and more, because it is not only an assault on the self but also on others. It has often been praised as a triumph over death, i.e. over natural death. Although some of these meanings of death and suicide appear incompatible they may coexist in a person's mind because attitudes to death are rarely unambiguous. Throughout life man wavers between accepting and denying death. It is one of the functions of religion to reconcile him to the inevitability of his own death and with the death of those dear to him. It is not at all clear what role ideas about death play in the motivations to suicide. They are interpretations of primitive impulses and fears rather than primary motives. It is remarkable that conscious preoccupation with notions about death is rare before suicidal acts, even among people who adhere to certain definite beliefs about death. Such preoccupation is more common *after* a suicidal attempt, for a short period at least. People who know that they are dying or contemplate suicide ponder the meaning of death much less than those who are close to them. It seems that the bereaved have a greater need for making sense of death and suicide than those who are dying or bent on ending their lives.

J. Choron suggested that the notions of death held by any person may be classified as potentially suicide-promoting or suicide-inhibiting. The notion of death as a kind of sleep, for instance, may be suicide-promoting. The above distinction did not imply that only pleasant and innocuous representations of death were suicide-promoting. For guilt-ridden persons the idea of eternal punishment may promote suicide, whereas for other people it served as an inhibitor. Choron proposed that the therapist ought to attempt to discredit suicide-promoting notions and that ideas about and attitudes to death should be explored in every case as a matter of routine, since such a procedure may have diagnostic as well as therapeutic value. However, he is doubtful about the possibility of manipulating the notions of death, in view of the frequent inconsistency in people's attitudes and views. He referred to an inquiry in which it was found that some people agreed with both the statements: 'Death comes to comfort us' and 'Death is the last and worst insult to man'. And he warned against taking it for granted that a negative attitude to life necessarily entailed a positive attitude towards death. This assumption seems to be taken for granted by the advocates of euthanasia (p. 133). Clinical experience does not bear it out.

Shneidman has proposed 'a psychologically oriented classification of death phenomena'. He wants to do away with the concept of death which he calls a semantic confusion and he proposes the term 'cessation' instead, i.e. the stopping of the potentiality of any (further) conscious experience. Different individuals, according to this author, can have a variety of attitudes towards their cessation. In their suicidal acts they may aim at one of the following: (1) *Termination* – the stopping of the physiological function of the body; (2) *interruption* – the stopping of consciousness with the expectation of further conscious experiences, and (3) *continuation* – these people do not want to embrace death but want to find 'surcease from external or internalized aspects of life'. They may kill themselves but have not necessarily 'committed suicide'. One of the difficulties of this kind of classification is the co-existence, or subsequent occurence, of all these notions in the same individual. And in most people they are much more vague than classifications such as those quoted above suggest.

It is doubtful whether notions about death play a significant part in the motivations to suicidal acts. Ideas and beliefs which one would expect to serve as safeguards against suicide are often swept away by others originating from mental illness or other stressful experiences. There is need for systematic research into this problem.

Suicidal acts have given rise to discussions not only on the meaning of death but also on the meaning of life. *Suicide and the Meaning of Life* was the title of a book by the psychiatrist Margarete von Andics published in 1947. The authoress was a pupil of Alfred Adler, the one-time associate of Freud. Contrary to Freud, Adler maintained that human behaviour was more strongly motivated by social aims and purposes than by primitive biological drives. Von Andic's clinical study was based on the premise that people committed suicidal acts because 'they have decided that their life is meaningless and that it should be brought to an end'. She arrived at the conclusion 'that the meaning of life, or its lack of meaning, springs in nearly every case out of the relations between the individual and his social environment'. The thought that he 'no longer fulfils a necessary place in the social community' drove the individual to suicide. Rendering service to the community in some form or other was the purpose and meaning of life. The quotations are from the preface written by Sir Cyril Burt, the distinguished psychologist. It is true that some people who commit suicidal acts explain them in this way in suicide notes and, in case of survival, in retrospect. These explanations are, however, attempts at rationalizing actions whose true motivations are largely unconscious. Normally, people do not ask themselves whether their life has a meaning and purpose and then decide to end it if they cannot think of a positive answer. If this was the cause of suicide the human species would long be extinct. Life has its own dynamics which are independent of social and other values. However, mental states which are associated with suicidal tendencies often lead to questioning and depreciation of values held dear by individuals and by society, and consequently to the feeling that life is empty.

The question of 'the meaning of life' is itself of doubtful meaning. Physicians and others concerned with the preservation of life are well advised to steer clear of it, lest they find themselves as judges of the worth of lives which they are called upon to save. They should beware of preconceived ideas about the meaning of life because such notions may severely limit their ability to help and may lead them into serious difficulties. At a recent discussion on the causes of suicide a Protestant clergyman asked what he ought to have said when an old and sick widow, who had lost all her relatives, and who was not receptive to the hopes and comforts of religion, asked him to tell her why she should not take her life. He was at a loss for an answer. Were there situations in which one had to concede that suicide was the only solution? The writer of this book had this to say in reply:

The question the woman asked the Minister might occur to most people in her predicament, but they do not usually press for an answer and go on living and suffering to the end. The fact that she did insist on an answer indicates that she was in need of medical advice. If she was referred to me I might tell her this: as a physician one observes that man does not stick to life because it has a particular purpose or because it is enjoyable. Although man endeavours to invest it with some aim and meaning, he behaves most of the time as if the preservation of life was life's main purpose. This is why something in you wants to go on living although you cannot see a special reason for doing so and often wish you were dead.

Such a frank and unsentimental affirmation of the life-preserving biological forces is often helpful to patients who feel that they have no longer a right to live.

People who are impressed by the apparently overwhelming logic and reasonableness of the motives for self-destruction in some cases, have to account for the absence of active suicidal intention in the vast majority of individuals experiencing similar or even worse situations. A famous surgeon used to tell his students how, as a young doctor, he was so sorry for one of his patients suffering from advanced cancer that he decided to help the poor man to bring his life to a peaceful end. The patient had asked him repeatedly to give him an injection which would relieve him from his suffering for good. One night when he had given the patient his usual dose of morphia, he left, apparently by mistake, the full morphia bottle on the bedside table. But when he called again the following morning, he was severely told off by the patient for his negligence. 'Think what could have happened if I had taken the lot.' This experience taught the young doctor that his patient's behaviour did not always follow the reasoning of the healthy observer, especially where life and death were concerned. Observations such as this have a bearing on the problem of euthanasia and it is not surprising that there has always been a lack of enthusiasm for this movement among doctors.

At first sight there seems much to be said in its favour, especially in our time when the expectation of life often far outruns the prospects of what appears to be a worthwhile existence. Yet euthanasia as proposed by its advocates is aided and abetted suicide decided in advance of the suicidal situation. Legislation making euthanasia permissible would in this country also involve the Suicide Act, 1961, which legalized suicide but made aiding and abetting it a criminal offence.

There is one motive for suicide which has not been discussed in this book, although it is invariably mentioned in popular discussions on the subject. It is pure weariness of life, *taedium vitae*. The reason for this omission is simply that the psychiatrist does not see people who are motivated by this mood alone. Whenever it is given as motive it proves to be either a manifestation of depressive or some other mental illness, or secondary to some loss, frustration, or affliction. Man does not weary of life without reason, and even if he does he does not kill himself unless other factors that have been discussed in this book are present as well.

*

Man's ability to take his life has often been acclaimed as one of the most precious human freedoms, even by people who have never comtemplated suicide nor expect to do so. Many, perhaps most, people derive comfort from the thought that they can kill themselves if life should become intolerable. It gives them the illusion that they are masters of their destiny. Helpful though this belief may be at times, psychological reality is much more complex than this thought allows for. Man has only a limited control over his drives, and they include his self-preserving tendencies. Nobody knows how overwhelming they may become under physical and mental stress.   *

The different sex incidence of suicides and attempted suicides remains still to be explained. Why on the whole do more males than females kill themselves and why as a rule do more females than males attempt suicide, at least in our society? The most common answer is that men use more dangerous methods than women and that therefore fewer men than women survive suicidal acts. If this was the whole explanation one would expect the total number of suicidal acts to be approximately the same in both sexes, after corrections for the size and age composition of the two populations have been made. However, the available evidence indicates that the total number of female suicidal acts exceeds that of the male. In other words, the excess of the female over male suicidal attempts is much greater than the difference between the number of male and female suicides. Males, then, appear to be more suicide prone than females, while the latter seem more prone to suicidal attempts. What might be the causes of this disparity?

Men, it is true, use more dangerous methods in suicidal acts than women, probably because aggression in males tends to take more violent forms than in females. (Most crimes of violence, including murder, are committed by males.) This does not necessarily mean that females are less aggressive psychologically than males. But why should suicidal attempts be more common among women than among men?

It is often said that women's attempts are 'less genuine' and therefore less serious and less frequently fatal. Only if one defines a genuine attempt as one in which the self-destructive component is strong enough to overwhelm the life-preserving tendencies can this be accepted. Women appear to use suicidal acts as appeals to the environment more frequently than men. This is the impression one gains from the clinical observation of large numbers of suicidal attempts. Women seem more inclined to use the suicidal act as an aggressive and defensive weapon and as a manipulator of relationships than men, probably because other means of exerting pressure, such as muscular power, are not at their disposal to the same degree as they are to men. The suicidal attempt is a highly effective though hazardous way of influencing others and its effects are as a rule more lasting than those of the physical violence that men prefer. But there may be still other reasons for the sex difference in the incidence of suicidal acts.

Professor Pierre B. Schneider of Lausanne relates the higher incidence of suicide among men to their greater vulnerability which he believes to be also manifest in disease and accidents. He regards it as a biological law that the male clings to life less and is less resistant than the female. Women's greater longevity – the life expectation of the average female in highly developed countries exceeds that of the average male by six years – can be seen as another illustration of this law. At any rate, from the biological point of view the popular notion of the male being the stronger sex is untenable, although it still holds true socially and politically in many parts of the world.

Suicide and other manifestations of violence. Pokorny of Houston, Texas, compared four types of human violence, i.e. suicide, attempted suicide, homicide and 'aggravated assault' to see if they arose in the same or different populations. Comparisons were made concerning age, race, sex, site of the act, and some other factors of less general significance. Suicide and homicide differed from each other in all respects except for sex, both being more common in males. Suicide and attempted suicide tended to occur at home, homicide and assault away from home. Suicide reached its peak over the age of 50, homicide in the late twenties, which is also the peak period for attempted suicide (p. 91). Suicide and attempted suicide differed in age and sex only, as had been shown previously. Homicide and aggravated assault, which corresponds to 'grievous bodily harm' of the English criminal law, were similar in all aspects studied. These findings supported the view that suicide and homicide were polar opposites if studied in large groups. The author conceded, however, that there possibly existed subpopulations within these groups which would be similar and he suggested that the homicide–suicide groups might be an example. D. J. West studied murder followed by suicide in England and Wales where the ratio of the latter to the former was 33:1. One third of the murders, which included those committed by mentally ill persons, were followed by suicide. The murder-suicides differed from the murders without suicide in that among the former there were many fewer cases with previous convictions and many more with a history of suicidal attempts than among the latter. In West's view, one in three murders can be regarded as extended suicide. He found that half of both the murder-suicide offenders and of the murderers were legally insane or could claim diminished responsibility.

15   Prevention and Prophylaxis

The ubiquity of suicide makes it seem inevitable. But it is difficult
to be defeatist once one turns from statistical data to the individuals concerned. In seeing the suicidal act in retrospect as the
climax of a crisis in an individual, one cannot help feeling that
almost every one could have been prevented. Compare accidents:
while it seems inevitable for a number of people to meet death
through accident, most individual accidents appear to have been
avoidable. This is why both the accident and the suicide rates are
a challenge to everybody concerned with the preservation of life
and health. They are equally difficult to reduce by planned action.

There has been no lack of recommendations how to reduce the
incidence of suicide. Low moral standards and the decline of
religious beliefs have most frequently been blamed for high
suicide rates. Durkheim did not dispute that religious devoutness,
irrespective of denomination, provided a certain degree of protec-
tion against suicide. He did not, however, attribute this effect
primarily to religious inculcations and prohibitions, but to the
fact that religion integrated the individual with a social group. He
regarded suicide as a symptom of a social disease. To cure it
society had to be reformed. This was impossible in the vast
organizations of the modern state. He recommended 'occupational decentralization' of communal life. He possibly envisaged
something like the revival of the medieval guilds. A development
in this direction has in fact been taking place recently and,
although the growing number of professional and trade organizations with local branches and international connexions serve the

power and prestige of occupational groups rather than the prevention of suicide, yet, by providing social organizations, they may be of some help. However, their scope is limited to people actively engaged in their occupations and they do not as a rule include the retired and the old. These groups present a much larger problem today than at Durkheim's time at the turn of the century when expectation of life was much lower.

Prevention of social isolation and integration of the individual with a group were in Durkheim's opinion the most important tasks for suicide prophylaxis, and all organized efforts towards agencies consisting of clergymen, welfare workers, and lay people have been formed to help people who have attempted suicide or are in danger of doing so. Ministers of religion have played a leading part in these efforts and medical men have acted as advisors. In this country the Salvation Army established an anti-suicide department as early as 1906, but its scope was limited to referrals from a few public agencies.

The first problem is how to establish contact between lonely people in despair and those who want to help them. If they do not feel sick and do not belong to a religious congregation, they are unlikely to seek medical or pastoral aid. It was an excellent idea to encourage such people to use the telephone for contacting somebody to whom they could speak in distress and despair. The Samaritans offer such a service to people in need of help irrespective of religious affiliation, if any.

The Samaritans are a remarkable organization founded in 1953 by the Rev. Chad Varah, Rector of St Stephen, Walbrook, in the City of London, a church with a very small number of parishioners. It was made known by the usual means of mass communication that people in despair and tempted to suicide would receive help if they rang the telephone number MANsion House 9000 at any time of the day or night. This attracted a growing number of helpers and clients and led to the formation of the nucleus of an organization supervised by a team consisting of two priests and a psychiatric social worker, with a consultant psychiatrist in the background. Branches organized on similar lines sprang up in many other towns and abroad. Membership is confined to lay people of all religions and of no religion. Originally, the direction of a branch had to be in the hands of a clergyman belonging if possible to the Church predominant in the area, but this rule no longer applies. For details see *The Samaritans*, edited by Chad Varah (1965); a new edition is shortly to be published.

The organization is based on the conviction that the majority of suicides present not medical but social and spiritual problems. The Samaritans try to help the person in despair, by offering to share and thus alleviate his burden. Only if the whole or part of the problem seems to be an illness will the client be referred to a doctor. The Samaritans' help consists of 'befriending', i.e. the offer of 'friendship, neighbourly care, concern, love by people who are lay both medically and ecclesiastically'. One quarter of the Samaritans are ex-clients. No attempt is made to force the client into a religious viewpoint.

The demand for help from the Samaritans is growing constantly. The number of branches in the United Kingdom was 134 in 1972. In inner London there were 9,000 new clients in 1970. Twelve per cent were referred to doctors. The organizers anticipate a big reduction of the suicide rate as the result of the Samaritans' work and claim a substantial share of the credit for the recent decrease of fatal suicide acts.

The Samaritans have become a world-wide movement and there are other independent lay organizations working on similar lines. All of them use the telephone as means of communication and offer, or plan to offer, a twenty-four hour service.

The principles underlying their work are in keeping with the findings of suicide research, but it will be difficult to establish in precise numerical terms what impact lay organizations such as the Samaritans make on the suicide rate. The incidence of suicide depends on a great variety of factors, many of which fluctuate. To demonstrate the effect of a particular one such as the work of the Samaritans, it would be necessary to keep the other factors stable, which is not possible.

What kind of people are the clients of the Samaritans? It has been shown in this book that people who commit and those who attempt suicide are two different though overlapping populations. Do the clients of the Samaritans belong to the former or to the latter, or are they a different group altogether? If they are, what is the risk of suicide among them? With regard to age and sex they seem more closely related to the attempted suicide than to the suicide group. The fact that they are seeking help may be taken as an indication that in the majority the immediate danger to life is not high, but it would be unwise to assume this. The clients of the telephone emergency service at Melbourne, Australia, were of the same type as the attempted suicides, but this may not apply elsewhere.

Bagley compared the suicide rates of fifteen English towns in which a Samaritan scheme had been in operation for at least two years with suitably matched control towns without a Samaritan scheme. Samaritan schemes were found to be associated with a reduction in the suicide rates in the towns in which they operated. The average change in the suicide rate in the Samaritan towns was a decline by 5·8 per cent, while in the control towns there was an average rise of 19·8 per cent. The Samaritans see very few of the old and sick who are so prominent among the suicides in the general population. Chad Varah believes that the very existence of a Samaritan branch in a community can prevent an individual from committing suicide. There is also a possibility that the emergence of such a group in a community is a manifestation of the presence of certain psychological and social factors which tend to reduce suicidal tendencies and which are absent or weaker in communities where no Samaritan schemes have been developed. Whatever the explanation, Bagley's study indicates that the Samaritans prevent suicide.

The Samaritans and kindred agencies are directed and staffed entirely by non-medical people some of whom have been clients themselves. Their approach to those in need of help has something in common with that of another lay organization offering mutual aid, i.e. Alcoholics Anonymous, whose membership consists entirely of clients. The emergence of these movements reflects a healthy tendency in our society towards the organization of self-help.

The participation of lay people in the prevention of suicide does, however, create problems which must be squarely faced. Uneasiness has occasionally been felt among doctors in case lay people should take it upon themselves, wittingly or unwittingly, to deal with clients who are severely depressed or otherwise in need of psychiatric treatment, instead of referring them to a doctor. The result of such misjudgements may be serious. This danger is obviated by carefully planned lecture courses on the causes of suicide which is part of the training of the Samaritans. Special care is taken to prevent the lay person having the feeling that he possesses expert knowledge.

What, then, is the role of the lay helper in suicide prevention and what is the doctor's role? There is a great deal of misunderstanding among lay people about the doctor's function. The following is a slightly modified extract from an address given by the writer of this book at the Annual Meeting of the Samaritans at Durham in 1962.

In offering help to those who contemplate suicide the Samaritans are trying to forestall the appeal effect of the suicidal attempt and indeed of suicide. They are trying to tell those people 'See, you can have friendship and love without risking your life.' You, the Samaritans look at the person threatened by suicide as somebody suffering from a deficiency disease, and you are trying to make good that deficiency, in the same way as the doctor treats a patient whose body has too little of a certain essential substance, by providing him with it. You are trying to offer love and friendship, the stuff of life which they lack. However, lack of a friend is not the only cause of suicidal intentions. There are quite a few others. This brings me to the doctor's role in the prevention of suicide.

I should like to discuss the following questions: (1) Who are the people in despair and with suicidal intention whom the doctor sees? (2) What does the doctor do for them? (3) Who are the people in despair and with thoughts of suicide, whom the doctor ought to see? I am not distinguishing here between the psychiatrist and the general practitioner. The doctor will, of course, see most of those who are physically ill. Physical illness plays an important part in the causation of many suicides, especially among the elderly. He will also see those who are mentally ill, although some types of mental illness, especially abnormal depressions, are not easily distinguishable from what the lay person may regard as a normal though somewhat excessive depression.

It is not easy to define what is the doctor's and what is the Samaritans' field of activity. What do we mean by mental or psychological illness? Certainly not only those conditions which used to be called the insanities. If we include the neurotics and the abnormal personalities as we must, we are dealing with large numbers of people variably estimated to form one tenth to one third of the whole population. Psychiatry used to be defined as the study and treatment of mental diseases. This definition no longer describes the scope of modern psychiatry, which is now more correctly defined as the study and treatment of abnormal behaviour.

What does the doctor, and especially the psychiatrist, do for those of his patients who are in despair and are thinking of suicide? Some he may have to send to a psychiatric hospital, but the majority are treated by general practitioners and in psychiatric out-patient clinics. Some are given physical treatments, many are treated with drugs, but most of them are receiving or ought to receive some kind of psychotherapy, which means that their individual problems are ventilated and the patients are helped in solving them. Whenever appropriate and possible, the doctor will gladly avail himself of the help of a social worker, of a minister of the Church, and of sympathetic relatives or friends of the patient. I cannot go into the details of the doctor's work, but I want to make it clear that it does not consist mainly of cutting, shocking, and drugging. In fact, what has been called the doctor-patient relationship is often the most powerful and effective method at his disposal. It plays a part in the treatment of every case whatever the illness may be. The doctor, then, is not an impersonal detached scientist as some lay helpers seem to think. It is true that his relationship to his patients must not become too personal, but the same is true for the minister of the Church and the Samaritans. All of us are, in our relationship to our clients, at the same time more and less than our private selves. All of us will get into trouble if we forget this. Nevertheless, the Samaritan who befriends a client enters into his life more directly, more closely and in a more practical way than the doctor normally does.

The third question was who the people in despair and with thoughts of suicide are who ought to be seen by a doctor. The logical answer is: all those for whom a doctor could do more than a layman. Everybody who is concerned with human relations can help those people as long as he is aware of his limitations. The Samaritans' main task is to receive messages for help from people in despair and to respond to them. In many cases first-aid will be sufficient, while others will require 'befriending'. It is important for the lay helpers to realize whose place they are taking in trying to help their clients. They are not standing in for the doctor nor for the minister of religion, but for a member of the family which acts as a source of strength and as a refuge in times of crisis. We can assume that if your clients had parents or brothers or sisters to turn to, or close friends, they would not have turned to you. If you define your role in this way, the problem which of your clients should be referred to a doctor or a social worker or a minister of religion, will be as easy, or as difficult, as it would be if the person concerned was a member of your own family or a close friend. In both situations you have to rely on your common sense and your intuition helped by whatever experience of similar situations you may have and what you have learned from others more experienced than yourselves.

Some suicide prevention centres are under the direction of psychiatrists and clinical psychologists assisted by social workers and health visitors. The personal Advisory Service established at Melbourne, Australia, under the aegis of the Mental Hygiene Department of the State of Victoria belongs to this type. There are now at least two hundred organizations wholly or partly concerned with suicide prevention in the United States, the most important at Los Angeles. There the Suicide Prevention Centre, financed by a Federal Government grant, was established in 1958. It aims at saving lives, at serving as a pilot project for other communities and at carrying out research into suicide. Its staff consists of psychiatrists, clinical psychologists, social workers, and a medical statistician. It works in close cooperation with hospitals and doctors practising in the city. It provides a consultant service to the coroner's office.

The Centre serves as a short-term emergency clinic. In two thirds of the cases the telephone is the only means of communication; one third are seen in face-to-face interviews. Special techniques for working with a patient by telephone have been developed. If specialist treatment is required the patient is referred to a hospital. Frequently the 'significant other person' over whom the conflict has arisen is involved in the treatment. The Centre has a twenty-four hour service, the nights being covered by suitably selected and trained auxiliary personnel. These 'clinical associates' are students from psychology, psychiatry, social work, and other related fields who receive some remuneration for the service they give. Contrary to experience elsewhere, the Suicide Prevention Centre has not found it possible to enrol voluntary helpers. According to Dr Farberow, one of the directors of the Centre, attempts at enlisting lay persons for work in this particular field have not met with signal success in the United States, but this difficulty is now being overcome. Voluntary work for social and other welfare agencies has, of course, a strong tradition in the United States.

The Centre has also taken on the task of informing and educating the general public about the problems of suicide through articles in the daily press and in magazines and through television and radio appearances of the staff members.

Many of the suicide prevention agencies mentioned above do not claim to provide more than an emergency service. Their function can be compared to that of hospital resuscitation centres for people suffering from the acute effects of severe poisoning. Today these units save many lives which only two decades ago would have been lost. Much of the work of the suicide prevention centres can be described as psychological resuscitation. They try to tide people in despair over an acute crisis and to advise them what to do to prevent further crises. Some centres offer expert psychotherapy to a few patients and the Samaritans aim at transforming the client's life situation by introducing another person into it. This is the nearest to an etiological treatment of the condition which led to the threat of suicide. All other measures are purely symptomatic, i.e. they deal with the acute manifestations of what often is a long-standing crisis.

Suicide prevention agencies can reach only a small minority in need of help. They are unlikely to reduce drastically the suicide rates. This can be expected only from *suicide prophylaxis* which begins at birth and even earlier. Its aim is to eliminate or reduce all factors which tend to increase the incidence of suicidal acts and to strengthen all those which tend to reduce it. The preservation of the family, active membership of a religious community or some other social group, the fight against alcoholism, good mental and physical health, good medical services, full employment, are all powerful factors against suicide. Divorce of the parents, physical and mental illness, alcohol abuse, widowhood, make suicide more likely. Some desirable advances may indirectly lead to an increase in the suicide rate. The triumphs of scientific medicine have benefited mainly the younger age groups and enabled more people to grow old and sick and thus more liable to suicide. Improvement of medical and social care for the old would make a noticeable impact on the suicide rate. A controlled study carried out by Sainsbury and his associates indicated that a Community Psychiatric Service tended to reduce the suicide rate among the elderly.

Is there a reasonable hope that within the foreseeable future the incidence of suicidal acts will be so drastically reduced as to make the loss of life and damage through self-injury negligible? This is unlikely at the present stage of human evolution while aggression remains such a powerful mental force. Aggressive tendencies, as have been shown in this book, play an important part in suicidal acts. They cannot, therefore, be viewed in isolation. Possibly, if they could be prevented altogether the incidence of aggressive acts directed against other people and objects may increase. The inverse relationship between aggression turned outwards and that directed against the self has often been noted. The invariable decline of suicide during war is probably due to a change in the balance of aggression.

Have we, then, to accept thousands of suicides and six to ten times as many suicidal attempts as features of our social scene? Certainly not, but the fight against suicidal behaviour is only one of the aspects of a much bigger problem which is the drastic re-orientation of society to the social needs of its members. Although suicides and suicidal attempts will continue to occur, it should be possible to reduce their incidence substantially. Improvement of the existing medical and social services could contribute towards this aim, but this is not enough. Social isolation cannot be treated by doctors alone or remedied by experts in social science. Besides, there are many more people in need of help than the professional helpers such as doctors, social workers, and ministers of the Church can deal with and, in any case, their scope is limited. What is needed is a mobilization of the latent resources for helping and healing in our society. This may sound rather vague and even obscure, but the idea of employing the unused therapeutic potentialities of a community is not new. Reference has already been made to the pioneer efforts of lay organizations such as the Samaritans and Alcoholics Anonymous, but they reach only a very small proportion of those in need of help.

The concept of the *therapeutic community* evolved by psychiatrists in the last three decades may show the way to a new orientation in social living. What is a therapeutic community? During the war, when the economic use of medical manpower was essential and time was limited, group methods of treatment for psychological disorders were developed and investigations of the patient community were undertaken with special consideration of the effects of the hospital community on the individual patient. The study of those effects led to attempts to use the hospital community as an active force in treatment. Not only had each member of the medical, nursing, and auxiliary staff a concept of his or her role in treatment and rehabilitation, but the patients themselves were made aware of the contribution they could make to the improvement of their fellows. Special attention was paid to communications within the hospital community and to distribution of responsibility. This approach to the function of the hospital group was a departure from the traditional notion that treatment is initiated, directed, and controlled from the top, i.e. by the senior physician or surgeon, and that all the others including the patients have to cooperate in carrying out what is prescribed and ordered by the highest authority. In the modern psychiatric hospital the rigid hierarchical organization has given way to the treatment team which usually consists of the doctors of all ranks, the nurses, occupational therapists, and social workers. Discussion and team work have taken the place of direction from above. The patients also play a part in the organization of the hospital activities, all of which aim at the alleviation of emotional tensions within the personality and in inter-personal relations. As the result of this reorientation the modern mental (or psychiatric) hospital has become a happier and more effective community than the traditional hospital run on authoritarian lines. Needless to say, the modern approach, though everywhere accepted in principal, has not yet been adopted in all mental hospitals in this country.

One of the leading pioneers of the utilization of the social forces within the hospital community has been the Scottish psychiatrist Maxwell Jones. He lays particular stress on the abolition of the traditional hospital hierarchy in which, in his opinion, the patient takes the lowest place of all.

Society at large could greatly benefit from the observations made and the principles evolved in the microcosm of the modern psychiatric hospital community. Probably the most important aspect of the new approach has been the realization that the doctor, to achieve optimum results in the treatment of psychological disorders, must integrate himself into the hospital community, all members of which contribute to the patients' improvement. But it is essential for each member of the community, including the patients, to have a conception of the role they play. Obviously, the senior psychiatrist's role is not the same as that of the most junior doctor or that of the staff nurse, but each of them is necessary for the hospital to fulfil its function and each of them can undo the other's efforts.

It is conceivable that similar functions could be organized in society outside hospital. The responsibility for those in need of psychological and social therapy would no longer be monopolized by the expert, as is the case now, but by a network of lay persons aware of their roles as helpers to those in need. The experts would, of course, contribute their special knowledge to the common enterprise. Thus society at large could become a truly therapeutic community. It may be argued that this is what happens in countries with highly developed psychiatric and social services anyway, but this is not so. It is true there are numerous public and private social agencies who come to the aid of people who ask for help, but their combined efforts amount to little in the face of the magnitude of the task, and they are too spasmodic. Also, their orientation and their limited resources enable them only to tide people over crises of which a suicidal act may be an alarm signal. They cannot create the psychological conditions which would prevent the occurrence of those crises. To do this society would have to evolve a new approach to social responsibility and a new social morality. The invocation of moral principles propounded by religious and other philosophies will have to be supplemented by the expert knowledge which psychiatrists, social psychologists, and sociologists have already to offer and which they will have to expand rapidly.

We hear a great deal today about the urgent necessity of scientific education beginning in the nursery and continuing throughout life. Only thus, we are told, can modern man fully enjoy the benefits of our scientific age, quite apart from the important considerations of economic survival in a competitive world. We are living in the age of a scientific revolution. At the same time, the incompetence of the human species in matters concerning the social well-being of communities is becoming more and more apparent. It is often said that things were better in the past, but this is doubtful. Even if it were true it would be largely irrelevant because modern society cannot be compared with societies of the past when the social problem of the aged, for instance, was relatively small owing to the short expectation of life, and when almost the whole of people's waking life was spent at work, which is an incomparable outlet for aggression. The progressive reduction of the working hours is likely to release an increasing amount of aggressive forces, only part of which can be spent on playing fields. Unless society learns to cultivate, from early age, the inclinations on which the positive aspects of social living are based, the outlook is very grim indeed. There should be no lack of time and of resources. In fact, one of the great worries of all concerned with social problems of today and the near future is the use people are making of their leisure time, and there is going to be more and more of it as automation gets into its stride. The planning, organization, and running of an all-embracing social service in which every member of the community plays a role which is meaningful to him, is the great challenge of modern society. Such a social service would have to provide for the deprived of all ages, that is for the child with a broken home as well as for the lonely widow. It would certainly reduce suicide proneness and suicidal crises, for we should no longer have to wait until a suicidal attempt mobilizes social or medical aid.

Today, social work is either a profession or a mission or a hobby. It will have to become part of everybody's daily life if society is to progress not only materially, but also psychologically. The principles, objectives, and techniques of social service will have to be taught side by side with those of science, beginning in the nursery and continuing throughout life. We must match the scientific and technological revolution with as revolutionary a change in social living.

Bibliography

ANDICS, M. VON, *Suicide and the Meaning of Life*, London (Hodge & Co.), 1947.

ASUNI, T., 'Suicide in Western Nigeria', *Brit. Med. J.*, p. 1091, 1962.

BAGLEY, C., 'The evaluation of a suicide prevention scheme by an ecological method', *Social Science & Medicine*, *2*, p. 1, 1968.

BOHANNAN, P., *African Homicide and Suicide*, Princeton (Princeton University Press), 1960.

BRUHN, P., 'Broken homes among attempted suicides and psychiatric out-patients: a comparative study', *J. Ment. Science*, *108*, p. 772, 1962.

CAPSTICK, A., 'Recognition of emotional disturbance and the prevention of suicide', *Brit. Med. J.*, p. 1179, 1960.

CARSTAIRS, G. M., 'Attitudes to death and suicide in Indian cultural setting', *Internat. J. Social Psychiat.*, *1*, p. 33, 1955.

CHORON, J., 'Suicide and the notions of death', *Proceedings Fourth Internat. Conf. on Suicide Prevention*, Los Angeles (Delmar Publ. Co.), 1968.

COHEN, E. A., *Human Behaviour in the Concentration Camp*, London (Cape), 1954.

COHEN, JOHN, *Chance, Skill, and Luck*, London (Pelican Books), 1960. 'A study of suicide pacts', *Medico-legal J.*, *29*, p. 144, 1961.

CRESSWELL, P. A., and SMITH, G. A., 'Student Suicide', (copyright), Cambridge, 1968.

DAHLGREN, K. G., *On Suicide and Attempted Suicide*, Lund (Lindstedts), 1945.

DONNE, J., *Biothanatos*, London, 1644, quoted from in DUBLIN, L. I., *Suicide*, New York, 1963.

DOUGLAS, J. D., *The Social Meanings of Suicide*, Princeton (Princeton University Press), 1967.

DUBLIN, LOUIS I., *Suicide. A Sociological and Statistical Study*, New York (Ronald Press Co.), 1963.

DURKHEIM, E., *Suicide*, (transl.), London (Routledge & Kegan Paul), 1952.

ETTLINGER, R. W., and FLORDH, P., 'Attempted suicide', *Acta Psychiat. Neurol. Scand., Suppl., 103,* 1955.

FARBEROW, N. L., and SHNEIDMAN, E. S., *The Cry for Help*, London (McGraw-Hill), 1961.

FIRTH, RAYMOND, 'Suicide and risk-taking in Tikopia society', *Psychiatry, 24,* p. 1, 1961.

FOX, R., 'Help for the despairing. The work of the Samaritans', *Lancet, 2,* p. 1102, 1962.

Proc. 6th Internat. Conf. for Suicide Prevention, Los Angeles, Suicide Prevention Center, 1972.

FREUD, S., *Mourning and Melancholia*, standard edn, London (Hogarth Press), *14,* p. 239, 1957. *Beyond the Pleasure Principle*, standard edn, London (Hogarth Press), *18,* 3, 1950.

FRIEDMAN, P., (ed.), *On Suicide. Discussions of the Vienna Psychoanalytic Society, 1910*, New York (International U. P.), 1967.

GIBBS, J. P., and MARTIN, W. T., *Status Integration and Suicide*, (University of Oregon Books), 1964.

GREER, S., and LEE, H. A., 'Subsequent progress of potentially lethal attempted suicides', *Acta Psychiat. Scand., 43,* p. 361, 1967.

HARTELIUS, H., 'Suicide in Sweden', *Acta Psychiat. Neurol. Scand., 32,* p. 162, 1957.

HASSAL, C. and TRETHOWAN, W. H., 'Suicide in Birmingham', *Brit. Med. J., 1,* p. 717, 1972.

HENDIN, H., *Suicide and Scandinavia*, New York (Grune & Stratton), 1964.

HENRY, A. F., and SHORT, J. F., *Suicide and Homicide*, New York (Free Press of Glencoe), 1964.

HUME, D., *An Essay on Suicide*, (reprint of the first edn, 1789), Yellow Springs, Ohio (Kahoe & Co.), 1929.

JAMES, W., *The Will to Believe*, New York (Longmans), 1927.

JONES, MAXWELL, *Social Psychiatry*, London (Tavistock Publications), 1952.

KANT, I., *The Metaphysics of Ethics* (transl.), Edinburgh (T. & T. Clark), 1871.

KESSEL, N., 'Self-poisoning', *Brit. Med. J., 2,* pp. 1265, 1336; 1965.

KIDD, C. B., and CALDBECK-MEENAN, J., 'Psychiatric illness in students', *Brit. J. Psychiat., 112,* p. 57, 1962.

KIELHOLZ, P., and POELDINGER, W., 'Pharmacotherapy of endogenous depression', *Comprehensive Psychiat.*, *9*, p. 179, 1968.

LENNARD-JONES, J. E., and ASHER, R., 'Why do they do it?', *Lancet*, *1*, p. 1138, 1959.

LUNGERSHAUSEN, E., *Selbstmorde und Selbstmordversuche bei Studenten*, Heidelberg (Dr Alfred Hüthig Verlag), 1968.

MALINOWSKI, B., *Crime and Custom in Primitive Society*, New York (Harcourt, Brace & World), 1926.

MASARYK, T., *Der Selbstmord als soziale Massenerscheinung*, Vienna (Konegen), 1881.

MENNINGER, K., *Man Against Himself*, New York (Harcourt, Brace & World), 1938.

MINISTRY OF HEALTH, 'Hospital treatment of acute poisoning', London (H.M.S.O.), 1968.

PARKIN, D., and STENGEL, E., 'Incidence of suicidal attempts in an urban community', *Brit. Med. J.*, *2*, p. 133, 1965.

PARNELL, W. W., and SKOTTOWE, I., 'Towards preventing suicide', *Lancet*, *1*, p. 206, 1957.

PELLER, S., 'Zur Statistik der Selbstmordhandlung', *Allgemeines Statistisches Archiv.*, *32*, p. 343, 1932.

POKORNY, A. D., 'Human violence: a comparison of homicide, aggravated assault, suicide and attempted suicide', *J. Criminal Law, Criminology & Police Science*, *56*, p. 488, 1965.

POELDINGER, W., *Die Abschätzung der Suizidalität*, Bern and Stuttgart (Hans Huber), 1968.

RETTERSTÖL, N., *Long-term Prognosis after Attempted Suicide*, Universitetsforlaget, Oslo, 1970.

RINGEL, E., *Der Selbstmord*, Vienna and Düsseldorf (Maudrich), 1952.

ROOK, SIR ALAN, 'Student suicides', *Brit. Med. J.*, *1*, p. 599, 1959.

SAINSBURY, P., *Suicide in London*, London (Chapman & Hall), 1955.

SAINSBURY, P., WALK, D., and GRAD, J. C., 'Evaluating the Graylingwell Hospital Community Psychiatric Service in Chichester. Suicide and Community Care', *Millbank Memorial Fund Quarterly*, *44*, No. 1, Part 2, p. 243, 1966.

SCHNEIDER, P. B., *La Tentative de Suicide*, Paris, Neuchâtel (Delachaux & Niestle), 1954.

SHNEIDMAN, E. S., 'Orientations towards death', *Internat. J. Psychiat.*, *2*, p. 167, 1966.

SMITH, A. J., 'Self-poisoning with drugs: a worsening situation', *Brit. Med. J.*, *4*, p. 157, 1972.

STENGEL, E., 'The complexity of motivations to suicidal attempts', *J. Ment. Science*, *106*, p. 1388, 1960.

STENGEL, E., and COOK, N. G., *Attempted Suicide*, (Oxford University Press), 1958. 'Contrasting suicide rates in industrial communities' *J. Ment. Science*, *107*, p. 1011, 1961.

STENGEL, E., and FARBEROW, N. L., 'Certification of suicide around the world', *Proceedings Fourth Internat. Conf. on Suicide Prevention*, Los Angeles (Delmar Publ. Co.), 1968.

Suicide Act, *1961*, 9 and 10. (Eliz. 2, Ch. 60), H.M.S.O.

TUCKMAN, J., and YOUNGMAN, W. F., 'Assessment of suicide risk in attempted suicide', in *Suicidal Behaviours*, ed. H. L. P. Reznik, Boston (Little Brown & Co.), 1968.

VARAH, CHAD, (ed.) *The Samaritans*, London (Constable), 1965.

WALTON, H., 'Suicidal behaviour in depressive illness', *J. Ment. Science*, *104*, p. 884, 1958.

WEST, D. J., *Murder Followed by Suicide*, London (Heinemann), 1965.

WEISS, J. M. A., 'The gamble with death in attempted suicide', *Psychiatry*, *20*, p. 17, 1957.

WORLD HEALTH ORGANISATION, *World Health Statistics Report*, Vol. 21, No. 6, Geneva, 1968.

WORLD HEALTH ORGANISATION, *Prevention of Suicide* (Public Health Paper No. 35), Geneva, 1968.

YAP, P. M., *Suicide in Hong Kong*, (Oxford University Press), 1958.

ZILBOORG, G., 'Suicide among civilized and primitive races', *Amer. J. Psychiat.*, *92*, p. 1347, 1936.

ZWEIG, F., *The Student in the Age of Anxiety*, London (Heinemann), 1963.

Index

Abnormal personality, 46, 62
  hysteria, 63, 103, 113
  psychopathy, 68, 95, 97
  See also Mental illness
Accidents, 53, 129, 137
Adler, Alfred, 51, 131
Africa, 21, 22, 36, 47, 65–6
  See also individual countries
Age,
  attempted suicide, 91, 96
  depressive illness, 61
  suicide rate, 25, 27, 29
Aggression, 13, 28, 52, 53, 60,
  126, 128, 135, 136, 145, 148
  catharsis, 117
  'death instinct', 52–3
  war, 26, 28, 128
Alcohol, and risk-taking, 125
Alcohol addiction, 53, 62, 63–4,
  98, 111
Alcoholics Anonymous, 140, 146
Andics, M. von, 131
Animals, 13–14
Appeal effect, 10, 113–16, 126–7
Asher, R., 103
Aspirin, 92, 93
Asuni, T., 36
Attempted suicide, 77 ff.
Australia, 21, 22, 140, 143
Austria, 21, 22, 27

Bagley, C., 140
'Balance Sheet Suicide', 125
Belgium, 21, 22
Bereavement, 47, 49, 61, 64, 114
Bohannan, Paul, 36, 65, 67
Broken home, 54–6, 61, 62
Bruhn, P., 54, 55
Buddhism, 67–8
Burial at crossroads, 7, 69
Burt, Sir Cyril, 132

Caldbeck-Meenan, J., 34
Capstick, A., 44
Carstairs, G. M., 9, 68
Causes of suicidal act, 46–57, 113
Choron, J., 130
Class, social, 26, 30, 33, 97–8
Cohen, J., 45, 124, 125
Cohort Studies, 94–9
  psychiatric observation ward
    group, 95–7
  general hospital group, 97
Comparative statistics, 19–24
  attempted suicide, 88–91, 98
Concentration camp, 127–8
Cook, N. G., 29, 92
Correlations with suicide rate,
  25–7
Cresswell, P. A., 34
Czechoslovakia, 21, 22, 48

Dahlgren, K. G., 18, 98
Definitions, 14–15, 77–87, 103–4
Denmark, 21, 22
Depression, 60–62, 95, 117
  'balance sheet suicide' and, 125
  case studies, 106–7
Divorce, 29, 42
Donne, John, 69
Douglas, J., 51
Dreaming, 62
Drug addiction, 62
  See also Poison
Dublin, Louis I., 23, 42, 73, 98
Durkheim, Emil, 7, 37, 48–51, 56–8, 137–8

Egypt, 21, 23
Eire, see Ireland, Republic of
England and Wales, see United Kingdom
Epilepsy, 103
Ettlinger, R., 84
Euthanasia, 133
Family, see Marriage and family
Farberow, N. L., 144
Female Sex, see Sex difference

Finland, 21, 22
Firth, Raymond, 66, 123
Flordh, P., 84
Fox, R., 37
France, 21, 22, 27
Freud, Sigmund, 51–3, 56–8

Gandhi, Mahatma, 67
Gas poisoning, suicide, 38–40, 42
  attempted suicide, 92–3
  case study, 96
Germany, 21, 22
  Nordrhein-Westfalen, 34
  West Berlin, 21, 29

Gibbs, J. P., 50
Greer, S., 104

Hara-kiri, 49, 57
Hartelius, H., 27
Hendin, H., 23
Henry, A. F., 50
Homicide and homicidal impulse, 28, 50–52, 58, 65, 136
  infanticide, 61
  suicide following, 47, 136
Hong Kong, 36, 42
Hospitalization, 88, 105–8
Hume, David, 69
Hungary, 21, 22, 27
Hysteria, see Abnormal personality

Illegitimacy, 29
Imitation, 56
Immigration, 36
Impending suicidal act, criteria for, 61
Impotence, 47
India, 67, 68
Infanticide, 61
Infertility, 47
Intervention,
  poisoning, 43
  suicidal attempt and, 82, 83–5, 101–3
Ireland, Republic of, 21, 22, 23
Islam, 68
Isolation, social,
  attempted suicide, 95, 111–12
  'broken home' and, 54, 61
  during suicidal act, 102–3
  impending suicidal act, 62
  suicide rate, and, 28 ff.
Israel, 21, 22, 27
Italy, 21, 22

James, William, 69
Japan, 21, 22
    hara-kiri, 49, 67
Jones, Maxwell, 146
Jung, Carl, 56

Kant, Immanuel, 69
Kenya, 36, 65
Kessel, Neil, 23, 104, 115
Kidd, C. B., 34
Kielholz, P., 62

Law,
    English law,
        prosecutions under, 7, 71
        punitive reactions of, 112
        reform of, 72
        Suicide Act 1961, 45, 72, 112,
            133
    European codes, 71
    Roman law, 70
Lennard-Jones, J. E., 103
Life assurance, 72–3
Lungershausen, E., 34

Male sex, see sex differences
Malinowski, B., 66
Marriage and family, 62, 93
    childbirth, 96
    divorce, 29
    suicide in family, 62
    student suicide rate and, 32, 35
    widowhood, 25, 95, 96
Martin, W. T., 50
Martyrdom, 53
Masaryk, Thomas, 48
'Meaning of life' and suicidal
    motive, 131–33
Medical care, and suicide rate, 28
Medical profession, 8, 30, 142–3
Menninger, Karl A., 43, 126

Mental disorders, 46, 57, 58–65,
    136
    depression, 60–62, 125
    mental hospitals, suicide in, 64
    schizophrenia, 62, 95, 97, 103,
        116
    suicide method and, 42–3
    See also Abnormal person-
        ality
Methods
    attempted suicide, 92–3
    suicide, 38–40
Monroe, Marilyn, 121–2
Moslems, 23, 27

National Health Service,
    narcotic poisoning and, 92
Negro, see Race
Netherlands, 21
New Zealand, 21
Nigeria, 36, 42, 65

Oates, Captain, 49
Occupation, and suicide rate,
    30, 36
Odlum, D., 72

Parkin, D., 91
Parnell, W. W., 34
'Partial suicide', 53
Peller, S., 81
Physical illness,
    cause of suicide, 47, 66, 107–8
    depression, 95
    primitive society, 66
Poeldinger, W., 99
Poison and poisoning,
    attempted suicide, 92–3, 104
    medical profession, 30
    suicide, 38–43
Pokorny, A. D., 136

Pregnancy, 47
Presuicidal syndrome, 60
Prevention, 137–49
    doctor's role, 141–3
Previous suicidal attempt, 62, 96
Primitive societies, 14, 48, 49, 65–7
Prison, 63, 85–6, 95–6, 127, 128
Prosperity, 24, 28
Psychodynamics of suicidal act,
    51–7, 121
    attempted suicide, 121 ff.
    catharsis, 117
    psychoanalytical contribution,
        25, 51 ff., 63
self-punishment, 117

Race,
    suicide statistics, 21, 22, 35–6
    U.S.A. Negroes, 21, 24, 36, 43
Religion, 26–7, 41–2, 45, 48, 62,
    68–70, 72, 130, 137
Retterstöl, N., 112
Revenge, 47
Ringel, E., 55, 60, 63
Risk-taking and the suicidal act,
    116, 121–5
Roman Catholicism, 23, 37, 50
Rook, Sir Alan, 32

Sainsbury, P., 29, 46, 47, 81
St Augustine, 68
Samaritans, The, 37, 138 ff.
Schneider, Pierre M., 80, 98, 113
Scotland, see United Kingdom
Seasonal fluctuations,
    attempted suicide, 89, 96
    suicide, 36–7
Sex differences, 25–7, 38–40, 47,
    81, 90, 91–3, 134–6
Shneidman, E., 131
Short, J. F., 50

Smith, G. A., 33
Smith, A. J., 154
Social mobility, 29
South Africa, 21, 22, 35
Spain, 21, 22
Stengel, E., 8, 18, 29, 92
Students, 31–5
    College system, 32
    comparative statistics, 32
    exams, 34, 47
    marriage, 32
    mental illness, 34
    separation from home, 38
    social class, 38
Suicidal intent, 77 ff.
    warning of, 43, 78, 86, 100, 113
Suicide notes, 43–5
Suicide phantasies, 53
Suicide Act 1961, 45, 72, 133
Suicide fashions, 56
Suicide pact, 45
Suicide Prevention Centre, 143
Suicide proneness, 54–6, 62–3, 103
Suicide rates, correlated factors,
    25–32
Suicide subsequent to attempt, 98
Survival, safeguards against, 43
Sweden, 19, 21, 22
    Malmö, 80, 98
Switzerland, 21, 22
    Basle, 43, 62, 89
    Lausanne, 80, 98

'Therapeutic community', 146–7
Tikopia, 66–7, 123
Trethowan, W. H., 154
Trobriand Islanders, 66
Tuckman, J., 99

Uganda, 36, 65
Uncertainty of outcome, 116,

Unemployment, 32, 47, 62
United Kingdom,
  England and Wales, 7, 8, 19–22,
    24–5, 30, 38, 44, 64, 88
    London, 29, 43, 46, 80, 89
    mental hospitals, suicides in,
     64
    methods of suicidal acts,
     38 ff., 92 ff.
    Sheffield, 89–91
  Scotland, 21, 22, 23
    Edinburgh, 23, 89
U.S.A., 13, 20–22, 23–5, 30, 34,
  38, 40, 42
  attempted suicide, 89
  Chicago, 29
  Los Angeles, 30, 44, 89, 143
  methods of suicide, 40–42

Varah, Rev. Chad, 138–9

Walton, H., 81
War, 26, 28, 48, 128, 146
Ward, Stephen, 122
Warning, *see* suicidal intent
Weiss, J. M. A., 116
West, D. J., 136
World Health Organisation
  (W.H.O.), 19, 21, 22, 24,
  38

Yap, P. M., 36
Youngman, W. F., 99

Zilboorg, G., 54
Zweig, F., 35